Falling in Love
When You Thought
You Were Through

Falling in Love
When You Thought
You Were Through

A Love Story

Jill Robinson *&* Stuart Shaw

HarperCollins*Publishers*

HarperCollins books may be purchased for educational, business, or sales pro-motional use. For information, please write: Special Markets Department, HarperCollins Publishers Inc., 10 East 53rd Street, New York, NY 10022.

FIRST EDITION
Designed by Joseph Rutt

Printed on acid-free paper

Library of Congress Cataloging-in-Publication Data
Robinson, Jill
Falling in love when you thought you were through /
by Jill Robinson & Stuart Shaw.—
1st ed.
p. cm.
ISBN 0-06-019864-8
1. Man-woman relationships. 2. Love. I. Shaw, Stuart. II. Title.
HQ801 .R598 2002
306.7—dc21   2001039959

02 03 04 05 06 ❖/RRD 10 9 8 7 6 5 4 3 2 1

This book is dedicated to our children:

Stuart Shaw, Jr. (in memoriam); Susan Shaw; Philip Shaw; Johanna Simmel; Jeremy Zimmer

and to our grandchildren:

Nathan Shaw, Kenneth Shaw (in memoriam), Tucker Shaw, Katherine Elizabeth Shaw, Justin Simmel, Ethan Simmel, Alice Simmel, Peter Simmel, Phoebe Zimmer

Acknowledgments

Mary Carwile, our dear friend, referee, and taskmaster, who gave to this book her judgment, energy, and tender loving care

*Falling in Love
When You Thought
You Were Through*

It's close to midnight. I'm alone in this dark Connecticut diner, writing here in the window by the desolate highway. I see his Jeep pull up outside. That Englishman, Stuart, comes in, places an order at the counter, and when he turns around to go, I shoot him this look, like 'I'm designed for you.'

He comes over and says, "Would you like to come to my place for a cup of tea sometime?"

'Round midnight. I stop by this lively Connecticut diner to grab a coffee. Across the room I see that woman, Jill, a writer, I think, amusing a pack of laughing friends. She catches sight of me and fires me a look that unmistakably says, 'Please come over'. I go over.

"Would you like to come to my place for a cup of tea sometime?" I say.

Part One

About Jill

"I Hate Sex." That's the story I was writing for *Vogue*. Sex had eaten up all my other drives, distracted me from my children, diverted my ambition, subverted my political energy, and tarted itself up as love, pitching me into two marriages, three selfish affairs, and lots of speedy bashes done by dawn in cars, on beaches, roadsides, desks, unmade beds in unmarked motels.

I never called love affairs relationships. That implied steely partnership, balance—no hysterics, no tragic endings, no despair—so how interesting could that be?

The Englishman was here at the ten o'clock morning meeting again this Saturday. I was sitting behind him. His blond hair rippled over his collar. He was clearly rational and smart. His well-worn, khaki workman's shirt was real, but he sat as if he was used to being in charge. Probably a manager.

I could wrap myself up, give him this fierce present of myself. He'd hear the time bomb ticking inside. 'Where do you put this?'

3

he'd say, 'It just doesn't go, isn't me.' He'd hand the gift back and run. It's easy to fall in love. Hard to climb out.

I looked out the window, across the highway to the tree-lined Connecticut road leading out to the house I'd just bought. This was where I wanted to be. I was forty. I'd learned all I had to know, and I was through with love. My best women friends had shown me how to pull myself together one more time. 'Push-ups, yoga, and tough deadlines will keep sex where you want it.'

I loved my best girlfriend, Josie, when I started school in West Los Angeles where I grew up. We'd stand together off to the side by the playground's ivy-covered wall, appraising newcomers. We knew we were different. It is hard to find someone as out of the ordinary as each of us believes we are—a condition we realize when we meet this special, private companion, the other side of the soul that makes the form complete.

If love includes magic attraction, jealousy, and possession, this was where that learning began. This was someone I couldn't wait to talk to, to look at. This was someone I wanted just for me. My heart jumped when she was on the phone.

How thrilling to glance at each other's smooth bodies on overnights. 'You have more breasts than I do.' Such a compliment. 'Yours will come, you'll see.' One night we tried on my mother's nightgowns. 'I'll wear the black lace,' she said, 'I'm more like that. You wear the pink.'

Our best evenings were spent lying sleepless, discussing what love might be and where it would lead. Same way kids sit up on the hillside, talking about their friendship and how they won't tell anyone, ever, about their secrets. They trade their best marbles or favorite crayons and nobody's ever going to know about this. And that's how it would feel on the first night you fall in love—the combination of going back to the past, that private, small place of childhood, and this huge, sweeping voyage of what would be the rest of your life.

Later, I used to take the Heritage Classics down from the bookcase in the living room. I'd slip the books out of their cases, looking for clues about sex—references to breasts, perhaps. The rough parts of *Leaves of Grass* I knew by heart.

At night, I'd wait until the house was still and my father had gone to his own room. It was stylish for married couples in L.A. to have separate rooms, like New Yorkers and European aristocrats. I'd go down the dark hall and tap on my mother's door. "What do you do with this pounding in your heart?" I sat in her pink chair, picking flecks off the painted-on silver flowers, sipping at just a touch of her sherry. I'd tell her all my crushes, like the one I had on Miss Lippincott, my art teacher. My mother was amused, never thrown. "Women often love women, and you probably are in love with Miss Lippincott's English accent." Yes, and her long, pale, cool hands.

Like getting a nose job, a convertible, tight slacks, or a bikini, going all the way was taboo. We'd made tracks into some taboos—seamless stockings, strapless dresses, sheath dresses, petting—above the waist. The romantic part of love was charming, softly lit, just like the movies. You'd send poems to each other, dedicate songs, and hold hands. He'd carry your books.

But I heard the other part could be gory, awkward; you'd be grabbed and turned like a calf wrestled to the corral's ground and branded, plugged, for how long and how exactly? No one ever made that clear, even though my mother assured me that once you got married, this dangerous, wicked thing would become 'quite beautiful.'

I expected to fall in love at the beginning of each summer holiday, when the aloof and intellectual boys came out from their Eastern schools to spend summers at the beach and around our pools. They took me to foreign movies in small theatres, and I gave the impression this was more interesting than watching the studio's dailies at home with my father. If I was going 'to find myself,' as some writers were putting it, I'd have to break away from home.

I had to be a virgin, but my mother said, "You don't want to marry one." Someone had to know what to do. "Here," my mother said, "you'll learn some other things you can do." She gave me her copy of *Lady Chatterley's Lover* and I fell in love with Mellors.

You could tell which girlfriends had gone all the way before they told you. You'd watch after summer when everyone came back from vacation or after a big holiday. It was there in the mouth, in the eyes, and the way they'd throw back the shoulders. They owned their breasts now, because they knew what they had and what it meant.

My father longed for me to become Eleanor Roosevelt, devoted to significant concerns. I longed just to be sexy and carry Lucite purses you could see right through. I wanted to feel arms around me and lips on mine. I loved the *idea* of someone loving me.

My boyfriend, Alex Glass, went to France one summer and smuggled home Henry Miller's *Tropic of Cancer* printed on long strips of paper. We sat together reading pages fast as we cut them, both of us more interested in reading how Miller wrote about sex than we were in doing it.

Alex was not only unpredictable, he wasn't into touching, and he wanted to be a writer, too. A combination that's hard to find or beat. With Alex I'd be part of a team, a woman out on the trail next to her man. When you fell in love, you'd love each other's work. Love meant sharing each other's days, having a partner.

My mother's parents ran a music school together, and my father's parents had a catering place. The school I went to was started by a couple, like the couple who built the hotel we went to in Palm Springs. And we knew couples who were screenwriters and songwriters. I wanted a man who wouldn't leave me behind each morning when he went off to work.

But Alex was killed in a car accident in Mexico. This, I explained to my writing teacher, was why I hadn't shown up at class. "You don't have to show up," she said, "so long as you're somewhere writing about it."

That summer my friends and I sat around making up lists of the types of men you could marry. Then we discussed which one was best for ourselves and for each other. A politician was perfect for me. There I'd be, by his side. I'm good in crowds. 'Except,' Josie said, 'you want to be the one running for office.'

A writer? I'd have my arm over his tweedy knit shoulder, consoling him as he wrote, bringing his scotch. 'But,' one friend said, 'you want to be the writer.'

'A businessman?' None of us knew what they did, 'and they're too neat.' And then, the wives of the studio stockholders and theater owners have to stand in the background, like politicians' wives, and parents working in the movie business wouldn't let us marry actors. If your mother was married to an actor, it would never occur to you that marrying one was a good idea.

The Englishman I was sitting behind at the A.A. meeting in the sunny room could be an actor, but actors are fragile. This guy was built like Picasso. Could be an artist, but his big, solid hands were too clean and smooth. The watch he was wearing wasn't a rough guy watch.

I touched him on the shoulder and asked for a cigarette. He handed it over his shoulder and didn't even look at me, which meant he'd noticed me and was already trying not to get involved. I've never been involved with a foreigner, but then, do the English consider themselves foreigners here? Or originators, and superior?

I never really fell in love with a man who had it easy. There always had to be challenge, a dark edge. Then, too, if he's already got a problem, there's maybe something you can do.

There was a reason for my first husband to need me and, therefore, to love me. "His father died when he was really little, and his mother's been married four times," my cousin had explained.

Alone with him on our first date, we talked about ideas and principles we shared. As we sat there in his mother's convertible, Jon said, "I don't know what we're going to do about this."

"Well," I knew, "we're too old to go steady, and I'm too young to have an affair."

"I guess we'll just have to get married." He radiated the sturdy security you wanted from the man you'd marry.

My parents would be delighted. They had struck magic, too, the first time they saw each other, when my father went to the Art Students' League and saw my mother standing at the tall, pine easel in her blue smock. My parents understood each other's creative work, and they had a spiritual match that kept them together through all the complicated years of their marriage.

Jon and I talked about our children, Jeremy and Johanna, how we'd raise them to have character. I'd make a serious leap into the world I'd seen when I baby-sat for my cousins, a world of Danish modern furniture and Saturday night dinners with beef bourguignon.

My father was waiting at the front door when Jon got me home at three in the morning. But my father would see right away this was perfect. Jon was Russian Jewish, his family was from New Jersey, and he'd lost his father so young. My father would mean so much to him. And Jon loved his singing voice, the idea of himself and theater. He'd be close to that dream world with me.

Does the man come with instructions, like the Sunbeam electric fry pan and the Mixmaster? 'You'll see,' my cousin explained, 'it's really easy, really fun.' I wanted sex to stay unspeakably private and sweet.

With marriage I could avoid going back to college. This couldn't be better timing. "He won't have the kind of money you're used to," his mother said. She'd sized me up quickly: a willful ingenue.

When you're a parent and you remember how you were when you fell in love, you know there's no point in trying to stop it: they'll grow into what they've done, adjust, and accept it. They'll hate you for stopping them (if you could), or not stopping them.

"But I'm different," I told her, "I'm not like that." I tried to recast myself as an earthy little homebody, my notion of his (or his mom's) idea of an ideal woman.

Perhaps he wanted a version of his truly epic mother, a powerful woman spilling over with expectations. She expected her son's wife to run his home the way she had, to be neat and organized. She eyed me up and down. "You'll have to work out a weekly budget. There won't be room for mistakes on Jon's Navy allowance." I'd be a manageable relief for him.

"Why didn't you stop me?" I later shouted at my mother, when after almost nine years I saw to it that my marriage was cracking up. I'd come to New York with our children. I said I was going to meet magazine editors—but I was running back 'home' to my parents, to New York, where they had moved after they left Hollywood.

"Imagine *me* telling *you* 'no,'" my mother said. She was doing a self-portrait against the Manhattan skyline studio in their apartment on East Seventieth. "Your father had a heavy Board of Directors on his back—and I was tired of keeping you from sleeping with someone."

"I wasn't going to," I said.

"You don't know that," she said firmly.

"I don't want to talk about that," I said. "This marriage isn't working. That's what I'm here to talk about."

"This marriage has worked just fine." My mother lit a cigarette. "You have two wonderful children"—I burst into tears—"and you loved him very much," she said. "Remember your wedding!"

I remember standing next to Jon's young glamour in his Navy officer's uniform. I believed I'd always have his big buoyancy with me. No question I'd be crazy about him forever.

Later, when I was alone with Jon at the Bel Air Hotel, I looked at him in the moonlight—long dark lashes, big firm shoulders. Could I carry this weight? Like Lady Chatterley, we made up names for the parts of our bodies, as if they were strangers we were introducing. What happened here should be, what? Choose one—thrilling? daunting? scary? Certainly not funny. Please, no jokes. I congratulated myself. I'd crossed the border, become the woman, and earned the ring. His mother's marquise diamond glittered on my hand.

We spent our first months in Coronado. I was a Navy wife. I'd spend my days writing thank-you notes I hoped my father would be proud of. My landlady tried to explain how you organized housekeeping. Jon was comfortable in the Navy. He liked the rules, the order, and for a while saw me affectionately as a sexy student. He'd eat frozen chicken pies I'd set out on our Tiffany plates. And he loved to see me waiting on the shore at weekends, waving bouquets of flowers as his ship pulled in.

When Jon was overseas, I went back home to live and work as a junior copywriter for Helen Gurley. She told me when my work was wrong, and how to get it right. She also told me you could work and have a man, too. "It keeps you lively for him. The last thing a man wants to hear about when he comes home is the washing machine," she said.

Women's lives seemed designed by magazines I made fun of, but I wanted to be the woman who read those magazines, to buy the right things, to keep the perfect house, serve the perfect meals, manage the laundry, hair, and smile.

"What is it you miss most about your husband?" Helen looked me over when we grabbed a bite to eat after work one evening. It was like a research interview. What, indeed, was this like, this being in love? I puzzled over Jon's letters, wondering. Helen was disappointed when I left my job after Jon came home from the Navy.

Jon became an assistant producer on *Leave It to Beaver,* and our life together paralleled the life on the show—affectionate, light domestic humor. Sex was an entertaining household product. You used it as part of a regular routine according to directions. Like the car, the clothes, and the help he paid for, it kept you turning out fresh shirts and good meals to keep your husband happy. We adored our children, but we had no understanding together, no agreement about how to raise them. To me, they were sidekicks, fellow explorers. I wasn't any closer to being able to put out order and discipline or to know what I really wanted than I had been when Jon and I met.

I was, however, catching on to a few more things I *didn't* want. I didn't want to be a Hollywood wife, after all. My mother and my brightest friends, the ones who left L.A. for the East Coast, hated watching smart women circling each other in lightweight hostess games.

My attitude wasn't helpful to Jon's work at the studio. I was an outsider, an observer. "You have to be part of the team," one of the wives told me, "you have to get into the game. It's good for his spirit, how he's rated."

Do you fall out of love with the person or with the scenario of your marriage? Did Jon and I fall out of love, or did wars over sex and money erode it? Did Jon's frustration over my vindictive extravagance come out in a kind of angry retreat, or was it frustration showing up on the credit cards? It didn't matter which came first. We were too angry, too worn out to care.

My marriage to Jon really ended when I thought I could afford to live my own way. I had published my first book, had a contract for the next one, and I had a radio show.

I was in love with the fast new L.A. art world Carla, my dying friend, was leaving behind. And I was in love with her husband's tragedy. Even now, I can see that look on Jon's face when he arrived one afternoon to pick up our children at Carla's house. I was serving pasta with her husband, Glen, and Jon saw then that our marriage was over. Jon was as loving as he knew how to be, and I despised myself, because he wasn't interested in the world I wanted to be a part of.

And then there was sex—a fierce, new subject with its own language and its own magazine. Helen Gurley understood women wanted to talk about sex: who was having it, why, and how you could have it, too. Maybe sex was love a day at a time. I'd never heard the word "orgasm" said aloud until Helen called and asked me to do a story about it for *Cosmopolitan,* which she was editing. I wrote "The Ostentatious Orgasm" before I could say the word or consider the sensation without a couple of drinks and a lot of chemical triggers. I didn't know too many women in those days who could talk to the man lying beside them about what was happening. The sixties had arrived with its open-door life: flowers in your hair, that music, those politics. You could sleep with anyone, be late, take anything—and in these actions, with this feeling in your heart, you were changing the world.

After Jon and I split, I went wild. I wanted to live in a Thomas Pynchon novel, and I did. When Carla died, I was the last thing Glen needed. I frightened him, and he began seeing someone else. I was shattered. "I have more than enough on my hands," he said. "How could I trust you, rely on you? You're ruining your life. I'm sorry." My difficulty, of course, was my own sabotage. Like every other failure in my life, I blamed this one on the man.

After the anger, there would come guilt, then rationalization. This was the Age of Aquarius, love free-falling. It never occurred to me to love any of the men I did sex with. Love was an adolescent fantasy.

Did I know myself well enough to trust any compatibility I thought I found? I went after love like a journalist goes for a story, but if the romantic love my parents had was my goal, was logic the track? Shouldn't love appear before me like a creature on a dark trail, as startled as I am?

I knew my second husband, Laurie, would be lovely company when I saw him walking up the road below my house in Santa Monica Canyon. I was writing, the kids were away at summer camp, and I was sure, maybe, this time I might not go out, might not drink. This time I would just work and go easy on the Dexedrine. We didn't call it "speed" then, but I had already figured out that these pills played with my fear and helped me hunt out the darkest quarries in every guy. I was learning that every guy's good side will be matched by the negative. An easygoing guy who makes love with such gentle imagination that the word "discipline" never crosses your mind, and never asks why you're late, is likely to show up late himself, lose things, and be casual about whether bills have been paid or not.

Laurie was pale as moonlight on a river, gently ambling there under the dark trees, winding up the steps to the door of my house in Santa Monica Canyon. He had a tall grace and such a sweet expression. The cigarette dangling from his mouth gave him a louche charm. He was exactly what I needed. A blind date. "Don't get involved," my friend who sent him to meet me said.

I was ready to fold into his lean arms before he said hello. Laurie made no demands, but there could be no demands on him, except total forgiveness. He had fast, long fingers and a mind made for math, poker, and getting out of tight corners. "Don't try to keep up with me," he warned, topping off the drink he always had in his hand.

Laurie applied his dazzling grasp of poker to all relationships and treated me with particular tenderness, figuring out how many moves he would take before he'd break away.

Some of us outsiders fall into a fatal chemical vortex, but only a few of us can reach up, grip the hook, and pull out. Laurie wanted the family he never had, he wanted us to hang on to him as much as he wanted to hang on to us. Just as he began to reach out, the desperate pull would come upon him and he'd disappear.

My children caught on when he'd be about to take off, and they'd sense when he'd be coming back, like cats sensing moon changes. Or, maybe, that's how I wanted to see it. He was the cat. He sensed when I'd be about to the end of my tether. They protected him from my wild attacks, even as they, too, were bitterly hurt to be left alone with my despair.

My closest friends, Joanne and Gil, hoped the wedding they gave us would set our lives on a new course. They knew I'd married the gift of a story that could have no simple ending, but does any life have a simple ending? Beginning? Middle? Most of the ten years we were married, Laurie was at war with himself. I learned you don't go into a marriage thinking there are things about the man you can fix later.

One summer, I left my kids with their father and followed Laurie to New York. We stopped drinking, and I wrote about how we saved each other's lives. The book's success made it possible for me to begin to reestablish a life with my children in Connecticut.

Then Laurie began to drink again. One night he took me to see *Farewell, My Lovely,* and the next day he disappeared. He called six months later to say he'd met someone, I'd really like her, and they wanted to get married. I reminded him he *was* married.

He had drowned my passion. I was done with love. Don't go close and you won't get hurt. I'd wanted the kind of equal attraction you see in the giant faces gleaming down from the old silver screens, where they hold the close-up long enough so you believe they'll die for each other, and the smoke from their cigarettes wraps them up together forever.

I'd quit love. Might as well quit smoking—next week. I lit the cigarette the Englishman handed over and blew the smoke softly around his shoulders.

Perhaps loving is an evolutionary process, and I'm not through after all. Maybe I've learned through trial and error to grow in my ability to select and to give. Maybe we have only one love story, and it's all about how our ability to love ripens, opens, and blooms. How rare it would be in the long lives we have now if the first person we love grows at the same rate, moves in the same direction. So, perhaps like parents, children, and buddies, our mates are but signposts on love's walk.

Part Two

About Stuart

"Last night I dreamt I went to Yorkshire again. I strode through secret dales and across brooding moors until I reached Robin Hood's Bay. There, on the windswept cliffs I looked out over the slate-grey sea toward a Viking homeland. The yearning to set sail into the northern sea was intense; so intense that I woke up crying."

"I don't know if anybody can make sense out of dreams," said Trenton, my mentor, "least of all me. But it sounds like you want to escape, to be somewhere else, like home."

"Perhaps the loneliness, I don't know."

"Of course not. How'd you expect to think straight after years of not thinking straight? It'll take a while. Stu, you'll have to relearn how to be a nice person, a regular guy who can take a girl out for dinner and a movie and not be obsessed with banging the girl's brains out or falling madly in love."

"Yeah, I may be through with that romance stuff, and that could be a good thing."

"That's projecting," said Trenton, scowling, "and negative. What I'm saying is that you've got to take it easy, change yourself gradually back into a human being, and then see what will be revealed. Meanwhile, keep in practice. Take a girl out for dinner. Take another to a ball game. If sex comes up naturally, okay, but don't make it the point of the exercise."

I'd been sober again for about a year, living alone, getting my act together in Southport, Connecticut, trying to revive a management consulting business, cutting out the booze. And getting over a disastrous affair with Zoe, twenty years my junior, a jazz singer I'd met in Chicago and deserted my wife and three kids for. Five years of magic and mayhem, sex and booze. Career and values all down the drain. Until one day I got sick and tired of being sick and tired, and I had to ask for help from people like Trenton.

But I'm ahead of myself already. Let me backtrack a bit.

I started out as an Englishman. Yorkshireman, to be more precise, which in London and the South already defines me as a barbarian. Since all evaluations in the British Isles begin and end with class classification, my background was such that if we're competing for the working-class, left-wing vote of approval, I had all the requisite qualifications. But if I aspired to middle-class acceptance, I could contrive a reasonable facsimile.

This apparent conflict became crystal-clear one summer evening in 1939. I was looking out through my bedroom window across the town where I spent my first years, Pontefract, or "Pomfret" as the old-timers called it. Down the hillside I could see the ruins of the old castle, and I could feel the history and the romance of it, reflected in the street names around the council estate. Cromwell Crescent, Fairfax Road, DeLacy Terrace,

Harewood Avenue. And I could imagine King Richard dying in his dungeon in the castle, uttering those terrifying words, *I wasted time and now doth time waste me.*

Across the hill on the other side of town was a castle and a prison of a different sort. The Prince of Wales Colliery, where Pontefract men had laboured underground year after year and where so many had died or been crippled in the mineshafts that ran under the park and the racecourse. The romance of the castle, the reality of the coal mine; it felt like a choice. At that moment I knew, deep down, that I had to choose the castle, choose the romance, not waste time nor have time waste me.

The very next day I was out in the front garden talking to a neighbour, when here came the school truant officer on his bike. Mr. Stubbs called me over. "Open this envelope," he said. "It's for your parents, but it's about you, Stuart."

A scholarship to the King's School! Visions of the school blazer, the cap with the metal badge and coat of arms, the two-mile walk to the lovely school with all its lush playing fields for rugby and cricket. Perhaps, most of all, it was not having to go to the Senior Boys School, which in my mind was a branch of the colliery where most of its boys were destined to work. I was on my way to the romantic castle.

My dad celebrated my scholarship by enlisting in the Territorial Army, a sort of National Guard reserve force. "A nice uniform," he said, "and besides, we'll be fighting Hitler before the year is out, so it's good to get in the army early." I fancied that, like many other men from this depressed area, he actually enlisted to get a steady pay packet.

It was a lovely summer. I was going to go to the King's School in September with all those well-off kids, and my father was in his dress uniform at the pub planning how to beat Germany. There would be a war "over there," across the Channel at the Maginot Line and the Siegfried Line. We would win, of course, because the sun never sets on the British Empire, and in geography class we were able to study the globe and see those huge patches of red, meaning British, on every continent.

Soon the Germans were invading France, but I was totally preoccupied with the sexual geography of the girl across the garden, Lucie, twelve years old, like me. We got together in the bathroom and touched each other, pressed gently against each other. I loved the curve of her sex and how neat it looked—there was no hair on it yet. And each time we played like this, I wanted to kiss it. And she liked it and I thought how the touch of it on my lips was so much like the touch of our lips on each other. This is what I knew was truly romantic, not the other things we heard about in the schoolyard from the older boys.

I spent some of my childhood living with my Grandmother and Grandfather Cawthorne in my Great-Grandmother Cherryholme's townhouse across from the Alexandra Cinema, which used to be a vaudeville theatre. This was because my mother had tuberculosis and was in a sanatorium for a long time. I had tuberculosis, too. The doctors cut out a gland in my neck, leaving a messy scar, and I was sent south to live for a while with an aunt in Portsmouth to get some southern sunshine.

My great-grandmother used to take me to the cinema just about every night of the week, usually double bills. After each evening's shows, we'd cross back across the street to the Queen's Hotel, where my great-grandmother would have a port and lemon and send a half-pint of shandy to me on the front step. The movies, the evening half-pint of shandy, and the morning fresh egg from the backyard hen coop imbued my great-grand-mother's home with the safe feel and comfort of pure velvet and chocolate toffees.

Life in my parents' home was less secure and predictable. Sometimes, the warmth of my mother's freshly baked bread. At other times, the fear when my father, in a drunken mood, would have me eat dinner with his favorite dog under the table. It all felt interesting then, and I didn't grow up harbouring any obvious resentment.

I was in love with books, with the Pontefract Library, and with Miss Rowlands, the librarian who had an encyclopedic knowl-edge of the book collection. She liked me a lot and would keep the latest H. G. Wells arrival for me. We were allowed to take out two books at a time, and I usually did this three times a week, so I got through about a book a day, except Sundays, which was mostly about church and the choir and being an altar boy and going to Sunday school.

I, like most of my school pals of that time, was mostly inter-ested in adventure stories, tales of exploration, travel yarns, mys-teries, and not at all involved in anything sexually explicit or daring. I was probably in my early teens before I caught up with Molly Bloom's soliloquy in *Ulysses* and Mellors in *Lady Chatterley's Lover*. Importantly, by the time I left grammar school to go to college, I had read most of what we call English lit and a fair amount of French lit.

More erotic than the library's fare was the cinema with its beautiful women in beautiful clothes, kissing and embracing handsome men. I wanted to hold gorgeous women like Hedy Lamarr and Paulette Goddard, Myrna Loy and Jean Harlow, and kiss them, long lingering kisses all over their bodies. Most erotic were the movie magazines, especially the *Lion's Roar,* put out by Metro Goldwyn Mayer's publicity department to its cinemas. An aunt who worked at a movie theatre in nearby Castleford would occasionally give me a copy, and I always felt she knew what I'd be doing with the magazine, especially the bathing beauty pictures, under my bedsheets.

My erotic education reached a peak when, in the early 1940s, some relatives, evacuees from the London Blitz, came to stay with my Grandmother and Grandfather Shaw. The relatives included a cousin, Julie, a year older than I, which seemed like a decade then. We fancied each other right away, and she brought me along at her speed, touching her all over and kissing Hollywood kisses every chance we had. Julie was hot stuff.

One golden afternoon we cycled out a few miles to Darrington Woods, pretty sure what our journey was all about. There was a wall around the woodland where we propped our bikes and clambered over into our own private glade. Julie looked like one of my movie stars with her long lashes and bright red lipstick lips. She sat down on the grass in the shade of a stand of beech trees, pulling up the skirt of her bright pink dress to show her navy panties that all the girls, including my two sisters and neighbour Lucie, wore. I lay down beside her and we kissed and kissed. Then she pulled off her panties and opened her legs wide, and I was on top of her for what seemed like the mixed-up time in an Edgar Rice Burroughs Martian story. It was forever: it was gone in a moment. All that remained afterward, and until this very day's memory, was and is no more than the time and space of the telling of it. Indeed, the preeminent sense of that everlasting brief encounter is that of a pink dress and then cycling home with no earth-shattering emotions after what, after all, was my loss of virginity.

Julie shortly after took up with a soldier from the Yorkshire and Lancashire Regiment at the Pontefract barracks. Then it seemed to me that Julie had lost her virginity long before me and that older soldiers were undoubtedly more satisfying than a virginal adolescent.

This first genuine sexual encounter generated a welter of confusing feelings. In one sense it was a turning point. I had "done it," the whole way, and my fantasy life now had an image from real life to focus on. But it had all been so quick, over in seconds. And there had been that fear. Girls got pregnant, and if you got a girl pregnant you married her. Abortion was rare among young women. Contraception was rare among young men and women. So this sexual experience didn't become immediately addictive. For some time afterwards, I found satisfaction in kissing and touching, adolescent groping, and then working these images and sensations into masturbating fantasies. The romance was in the chase; the poetry was in the unrealised yearnings; the woman was idealised and unobtainable, and thus unsullied.

I'd gone over to the Sherwood Diner after the Wednesday night twelve-step meeting, and over coffee and a burger got into conversation with several people from the program and a girl called Jill. The talk turned to writing, which interested me as I'd been writing short stories for a long time and had embarked on a novel.

I'd seen this woman, Jill, before at local A.A. meetings. She struck me as the neurotic type, very intense, with sometimes a scared animal look on her face, powdered in a hurry, like the rough powdered skins of women you see in Yorkshire early in the morning as they hurry off to jobs in the mills, the factories and shops.

She was articulate and original, and she aroused a vague empathetic feeling in me. This feeling runs smack into my mentor's caution a few days ago that 'under every skirt there's a slip'; slip meaning relapse. So I said good night to the gang and drove down to Dameon's, a jazz joint in Westport where my friends, John Mehegan and Linda Pomerantz, were playing four-handed jazz piano. I ordered my ritual Coke and lit a Marlboro, soaking up the jazz. John joined me for a drink.

"You missing Zoe?" he asked.

"Yeah, a little, but there's no future there, you know that."

"But a great gal and a good singer, and she must be hot stuff in the sack, twenty years younger and all that jazz."

"Yeah. See you later," I said, and drove back to my house in Southport and the lonely night.

I'd met Zoe in Chicago in the Old Town Ale House on North Avenue, and it was sex at first sight. She was dancing by herself to the jukebox and I joined in, which led to drinks and more drinks, then to Mr. Kelley's, Figaro's Lounge, Eddie's, and the Back Room, ending up drinking after hours in an Italian joint. We took a room at the Lake Shore Hotel and made love until dawn and into the following morning. That was the beginning of a consuming affair that lasted five years.

Zoe suited me perfectly because all she wanted to do was sing and dance and party and would make love at the drop of a hint. This was not new behaviour for me, simply an acceleration of a promiscuous lifestyle I'd adopted years earlier. My sense of responsibility, of morality, all went out the window and I was lost in a fog of alcohol, increasingly unfunny fun, and increasingly desperate and unfulfilling sexuality.

I was a disaster waiting to happen. I had drunk my way out of a brilliant career at Procter & Gamble in Cincinnati and had split to go work for Hugh Hefner in Chicago. My arrival at Playboy was heralded in the press as a clear case of Hefner recruiting a "blue chip" executive to help launch Playboy Enterprises on the stock exchange. I lasted about six months before I quit: it was like oil and water.

So here I was in Chicago in a penthouse on Lake Shore Drive with my wife and kids just moved up from Cincinnati, and I was out of a job. But everything would be just fine because I would now become the greatest marketing consultant in the Western world. Besides, I had money in my pocket.

I deserted my wife and children and flew to Jamaica with Zoe for a few weeks of pure hedonism. It was a haze of beach parties, Blue Mountains, Rastafarians, white rum, and gange, all to the incessant beat of Bob Marley. When I got back to Chicago, my family was gone, the penthouse empty. A marriage of twenty years was over. I had blown it. And I didn't care.

My world fell apart. The decline was printed in the addresses, from the Lake Shore penthouse, to a rental at the Churchill, to a hovel somewhere. To Zoe's parents in Michigan. To a rehabilitation centre in Racine, Wisconsin.

So I'm rehabilitated and making a fresh start with a high-powered consulting assignment in New York. I took a house in Southport, Connecticut, and moved in with Zoe and her two kids. I was no longer the party boy and Zoe was still a party girl, so inevitably we split. This is how I found myself alone in this house trying to put a life back together.

Soon I would have a companion for a couple of weeks. My ex-wife was coming to stay with me and recuperate from some minor surgery. We'll drive around, probably go down to New York City, catch some theatre, have fun, talk about our children—Stuart Jr., Susan, and Philip. We'll probably get along fine. I care for her and regret deeply all the wrongs I did her. I love her still, but we won't sleep together. It will be not at all complicated.

Margaret is still on my mind as I wrestle with sleep. And inevitably, I drift back to the woman I forsook for Margaret. Danielle.

I have never been more passionately in love than with Danielle, although I recognise now how place, time, circumstance, and innocence conspired to glamourise the love affair— that first, fine careless rapture.

It was 1947, and I'd been awarded a grant to study anywhere in Europe through the summer. My choice was entirely governed by an assessment of the food situation in various university cities. To hell with academia: I was hungry. Switzerland was by far the best bet, and the University of Lausanne took me in. I knew I'd made the right choice when the train hit the Swiss border and the platform was alive with chocolate vendors, their trays overflowing. No ration book. I ate my way through the semester.

Danielle was an American, home in Manhattan, origins in Switzerland, and Germany before that. Danielle Cohen, penetrating eyes in a beautiful face, a voluptuous long-legged body suggesting passionate sexuality, a mixed-up speech pattern from her mixed-up upbringing, and, most of all, a sensuous, exotic presence and a deeply romantic nature. We fell for each other in an instant.

That mad rush of fierce romantic love has had a thousand descriptions, all of them clawing at the indescribableness of the sensations. We resort to metaphor, and the metaphors are individual, not transferable, as elusive as the descriptions of perfumes.

Danielle, I discovered quickly, was all about meaning, particularly meaning as revealed by art and literature. This was the bond, the instant and deep attachment as we soared through shared experiences of painters, writers, musicians. Conversation was a euphoric addiction, the raw sexuality assigned a subsidiary role. We immersed ourselves in music and dance, and poetry above all—Eliot, Spender, Rilke, Rimbaud. I wrote a poem for her every day, and we reached an emotional climax, the "I love you" moment, in a record booth in a music shop off the Grand Chêne, listening and holding hands to the music. Debussy's "L'Après Midi d'un Faune."

Here in Connecticut tonight, decades later, I could still be moved by this music. I went downstairs and played it again, and the tears, as always, overflowed. I'd heard that sentence so often, 'You'll get over it.' It's just not true. With a great passion, you never get over it. It eases down, but it never goes away, and right now some of those original feelings from that summer long ago play again in the Debussy lushness.

Words are hard to come by to describe this passion of mine for Danielle and hers for me. It was so very romantic in all the obvious clichés; embracing, kissing, tangoing, talking of life, literature, and love and music the way nineteen-year-olds do. We knew we had these wondrous, powerful feelings for each other, but they did not translate directly into sex. We did not make love: we were too much *in* love. Perhaps too much in love with the romantic images of ourselves. Perhaps in love with being in love.

That Christmas, Danielle said she couldn't bear to be apart, and she was coming to London for ten days, which we should spend together. Oh yes, my heart leaped, and I felt good that I'd been faithful to her, telling everybody at college that I'd married Danielle that summer in Lausanne.

We found a place to stay in London, Bloomsbury of course, and spent a week of adventure in theatre, cinema, galleries, and bed. Actually most of the time we spent talking and writing. All those nights in bed together, endless foreplay, but never a consummation. Either we were too romantic for actual sex or too frightened of what it might lead to.

On the platform of Victoria Station, Danielle leaned out of the carriage window, waving as the train edged away, the steam blowing over her face and long, dark hair. Danielle disappearing into a mist, back to Lausanne. I thought only of when I would see her again.

We didn't see each other again. In the summer of 1948, when we'd contemplated marriage, Danielle was back in the U.S.A., and I was in Budapest, writing about life behind the Iron Curtain for a British newspaper chain.

Danielle was on my mind this morning as I walked down to Southport Harbor to meet Trenton for coffee and smokes at the little Main Street café. Perhaps not Danielle so much as the transition from Danielle to the woman I married, Margaret Anderson, and how badly I felt about my marriage breakdown.

"I guess I'm feeling guilty about what I did to Margaret," I said, "all the drinking and messing around, and occasional violence."

"You have to live with that," said Trenton, "but one day soon, you'll have to make amends to Margaret. That's part of getting straightened out. It's mostly about honesty, and honesty is the bedrock of your spiritual life. How about some more coffee?"

Twenty years I had spent married to Margaret Anderson and that ended ten years ago, so I found it hard to recapture the truth of what our relationship was all about.

I had fallen in love with a graceful, beautiful, and stylish young woman, who first caught my eye standing in a line in the college refectory. She wore a form-fitting beige sweater and a plaid "New Look" ankle-length skirt, which was all the rage then. The skirt was belted at an incredibly tiny waist, which—I found later—I could span with my hands. Ankle-strap high heels completed the look, and they threw her back with her head held high and her long chestnut hair about her shoulders. And, so fittingly I thought, a cigarette in her fingers. An adolescent Bette Davis.

"She's the college administrative assistant helping the president of the Student Union," my pal informed me. "She's very active politically, a Young Conservative, and she's going out with a tall, handsome Dane who is almost as well-dressed as the rich Persian students. Best of luck."

I didn't need any luck. That afternoon, I asked her if she would mind typing some material for me for the Student Union and she said, "Of course, and perhaps you'd like to take me to the Catholic Ball next Friday night." No-nonsense woman!

The Catholic Ball was to prove a turning point in my life. Margaret and I had a few drinks, danced madly all night long, and won the dance competition, a bottle of champagne. A little tipsy, we left the ball and repaired to my college newspaper office where we made love. It was like breaking a dam with torrents of pent-up passion pouring through, the Danielle celibacy and pristine romance swept away into an erotic maelstrom. If sex can be an addiction, this is precisely when my addiction began. Margaret liked it and this seemed a revelation, as though for the first time I felt like a partner, not an aggressor. So here was my woman, beautiful and smart, stylish and sexy. She drove Danielle completely out of my mind. We made love at every opportunity and hurtled into an engagement.

Margaret accompanied her parents to Washington, D.C., to help them get established when they emigrated to America. She had a good job working for the former Secretary of the Interior, Harold Ickes. She came back to England after a year to marry me and spend the next three years as the wife of Flying Officer Stuart Shaw and the mother of Stuart Shaw, Jr.

After I left the R.A.F., we moved to Washington, D.C., where I worked as a journalist and for the British Information Service during the Army-McCarthy hearings. Lured by a fatter pay-cheque, I shifted to a management career at Procter & Gamble in Cincinnati. This life seemed to suit Margaret. She was partner to a man who was setting a track record at his company, and we were soon able to buy a car and then a house, and eventually a lavish estate. Our first child was joined by a beautiful sister, Susan, and a handsome brother, Philip. Wonderful, strong, healthy children.

The dark side of our life together became my progressive drinking, associated with progressive promiscuity. We didn't talk. I mean really talk, not just conversation, the weather, the dog, the dinner party, but honest and willing talk about our dreams and aspirations, what was in front of us beyond another promotion, another title, another stock option. We didn't talk about sex, even though sex had been such an important element of our love affair. As time went on and my promiscuity became an open secret, we had no way to get over the barriers of bitterness and guilt.

We retreated into our fortresses of denial and complaint. My work, particularly, was stressful, highly competitive, requiring long hours and endless travel around the country. The old, old story. A man beats his brains out all week and comes home on Friday night, projecting a gorgeous wife standing on the doorstep, wearing a black bra and panties and high heels, and a shaker of martinis in one hand and a glass with a twist of lemon peel in the other. 'Welcome home, lover . . .' And the reality is kids and shopping and 'Let's go out for dinner tonight.'

It was inevitable, the collapse of values, the erosion of structure as love gave way to lust, sensibility to sensation, truth to lies, or, as my dad used to say, "believing your own propaganda." The marriage ran out of compromises.

I was taking Trenton's advice and keeping in practice, dating an assortment of interesting women. But I was disengaged, sociable but distant. I began to feel that my romantic flame had gone out and that sex, occasional as it now was, had become routine and passionless. I wondered what my responses would be when Margaret came to visit me in a couple weeks' time.

One

"I'd been wandering from saloon to saloon, gulping vodka all day long, looking for my girl, Zoe, going crazy with worry about her. Some kind of trouble. Somehow I worked my way back to our apartment. No Zoe. More vodka. Pass out.

"Then she was there, drunk, stoned, screaming at me and hiking her skirt up around her haunches. 'I couldn't find you,' I yelled, 'where the hell were you?' 'I went out on you,' she taunted me, 'I fucked a lonely football player, so fuck you.'

"My head exploded, I grabbed my fish-scaling knife, and slashed her across her thighs. Then I must have fallen down, knocking over a lamp. The next thing I remember, the room was full of Chicago cops, something was burning, and I saw blood on Zoe. I'm being handcuffed. So is Zoe. And I'm shouting at the cops, 'Don't do that to her, she hasn't done anything. It's all me, it's all my fault.'"

What I heard, behind the tough facts, was simple. Here was a man filled with passion, but he'd been betrayed, hurt. I understood betrayal, understood being hurt. I remembered leaping at Laurie when he'd come back after weeks away, bashing him with my fists. This man was deep, looking at himself with a new perspective, reflective, but not bitter.

English, blond, a big story. I grabbed my friend Pat's arm. "He's designed for me," I told her.

I talked quickly about his look, his voice, his accent. It was easy to fall for the glamour of his story, but what I caught was his capacity for devotion. This is what I knew I had, too. He had the modesty of an assured character who knew without question that he could change. When you stripped it all away, standing up here was a man who was capable of commitment.

"We knew you'd see Stuart." Then she repeated, "I'm serious. Stay away. He's trying to make it this time."

I hadn't been looking for the Englishman when I realized I was sitting behind him again this morning. The early light came through the windows of the old church stable, casting his shape into appealing broad planes.

I tapped him on the shoulder to ask for a cigarette.

"Could you spare one of your Marlboros, please?" The voice from the row behind me was American, possibly California, a little Lily Tomlin. Great voice-over voice. Pity cigarette TV commercials are gone now. Imagine: 'Could you spare one of your Marlboro Men, please?'

Must be that woman who came into the meeting room with Pat, the counselor from the Norwalk Hospital Psych

Ward. Addict? Alcoholic? Or everything, including nicotine.

I passed the pack back over my left shoulder, not saying anything but "Yeah." The lighter's click, and then a stream of smoke back over my right shoulder. Did this qualify as a "pass"?

"Her name is Jill," a friend told me the next evening.

"I've seen her around the meetings," I said. "She seems to be articulate," I added.

"She's some kind of writer," my friend said, "kids' books, I think. Bedtime stories."

It was a soft summer night, and I stopped by the diner to work on my new book about this woman who goes out with a young rock singer and, as her son says, gets better tickets to concerts than he can.

The rock singer I had been going out with was dying of AIDS. America's brief period of liberated sex was, literally, dying out. Sex as entertainment, as artistic exercise, as therapy, hadn't done much for romantic love. I worked out a dozen ways to place the encounters outside guilt's range.

My son and daughter were out with friends. I liked it when they were home, their books and papers mixed up with mine, their music playing, and I could make supper for everyone. I liked our house to have a kind of commune feeling. 'If,' Johanna said, 'Ralph Lauren did communes.'

If love means giving, I was certain I wasn't going to meet anyone to love. Who would give in to life as the three of us have designed it? A house filled with our friends and pets, our books, our sound, our art. We had it our own way.

I was sitting by the window at the diner. Nothing catches solitude better than your own reflection in a fairly empty diner, against the bleak, moving backdrop of a night highway shot by lines of speeding headlights. I say I hate to be alone, but I love this time.

I hadn't ordered anything, just coffee. Hunger gives my writing edge.

After the Friday night meeting, I drove over to the diner on the Boston Post Road, planning to pick up a girl who said she'd like to go hear jazz with me at Dameon's in Westport. My friend John Mehegan's playing there. The girl can't make it, baby-sitter problem.

From the window of the diner, I saw the Wagoneer make a scary bolt of a turn from the far lane across an alarmed brace of oncoming cars, and dip and plunge into the parking lot. The Englishman had his arm out the window, the sleeve of the khaki shirt rolled up.

I looked at the clock high up over the coffeemakers. Ten forty-five. Did he have an early date? Or he may have a late date.

He looked serious and determined. The horn-rimmed glasses gave a fierce frame to stern blue eyes. He wasn't a man who wanders by, drops in, then figures out what he's doing.

He went to the counter and placed an order to go. He was meeting someone. He held his cigarette between his thumb and forefinger, drawing it out slowly. He wanted coffee for the long drive into New York. Of course, he'd be involved with someone in New York. The singer, the girl he stabbed. She'd likely be in

New York. You can't make love work out after something like that. I could tell them that. Once there's been violence, betrayal, abandonment (especially that), you know you're just waiting for the next time.

He wrapped paper napkins around the coffee and turned to the door. He saw me. How could he not? I might have been standing up, waving my arms for all the verve and luster I pitched into this expression. This look must say, 'I am made exactly for you, I am everything you'll ever long for, ever need. See me! I am wild for you!'

There was no comic instant of looking around—'Does she mean me?' In that moment, in that diner, on that planet, there were no other creatures, no other living spirits.

Too slowly, with such deliberate steps, he came over to my table. I bolted myself to the seat. Not yet, I told myself, not yet can you run to him in slow motion across the screen. We'll have that later. Such confidence, to think *we!* He stood right next to me, looking down, coffee cup in hand, both of us doing "hello" without a cigarette.

I glanced across the crowded room and something odd happened. I saw Jill with a tableful of guys, with her face shining at me as though spotlighted, highlighted. Everything else shifted out of focus and became a dark background to her face.

I went over to the table where she was sitting. Jill's eyes were on me. What do I say? "Haven't I seen you around? A meeting or something?"

"Yes," she said.

"You write children's books?" I asked.

"Are you thinking of *Bed/Time/Story?*" she said. "Not exactly for kids."

"Would you like to come to my place for a cup of tea sometime? I live close by in Southport."

"Right now would be good," she said.

"That's okay with me, but right now I'm on my way down to Westport to hear some guys I know play jazz," I said. "You could come with me, and I'll bring you back to your car."

"Perfect," she said, "I'm crazy about jazz!"

As we entered the chatter and smoke of Dameon's, John Mehegan broke into "April in Paris." "My signature tune." I smiled at Jill. "He always plays this when I come in."

What I really should have said was that John had been playing that tune—shades of Count Basie, "One More Time"—since Our Paris Experience, as Mehegan referred to it.

It was last year, approaching my birthday in April. John and I were having a few cocktails in a Manhattan lounge when the idea came up of some kind of birthday treat, which finally modulated into an April in Paris birthday treat. "We'll do it," I said, and got on the phone to my travel agent. The next day we were aboard the Concorde and enjoying birthday champagne and caviar.

We didn't stay long in Paris, just a few days at the George V. Meals, jazz joints, and lots of drinking. We befriended a guy who said he was the driver for an Algerian rebel, so naturally I hired him on the spot to drive us to the South of France. I have a vague recollection of pausing for a meal in a Michelin-starred restaurant in Lyons, where John shamed us by insisting on "thick soup." The driver was a maniac in the big rented Mercedes, and must have set the land speed record for the run from Lyons to the

Côte d'Azur. I don't remember it. Only my American Express bills remembered the adventure.

When I reconnected to the known universe, I found myself sitting at a blackjack table with a huge pile of chips in front of me. Why, I'd asked myself, are they all speaking French? They were speaking French because I was in a Salon Privé of the Monte Carlo Casino and several thousand francs ahead. My God, where was Mehegan? I found him at the piano with the casino band playing "'Round Midnight." It was a good evening.

"We had a neat visit to Paris," I told Jill, "had a hell of a good time. That's why it's my signature tune!"

John and Helen doing four-handed piano were hot tonight, and Jill seemed to dig it. Jill was delighted to be included, part of the gang already. I noted that I'd excluded any mention of Zoe being on the Paris jaunt with us. Playing up to Jill, I guess.

Going to jazz clubs in the Village, in Hollywood, and in Venice Beach had nothing to do with music and everything to do with the men. Men who love jazz are more inventive lovers, languid, capable of hanging on to any beat your body has in mind and into all-night sessions. Some of these could be all-night drinking sessions or poker sessions, but when you are a novel distraction, their riffs are limitless, as blue and dark as the deepest club lighting.

Dameon's, a dingy little club by the Westport railroad station, had a small table for Stuart up front with a couple of his friends. Helen, one of the musicians, gave me a cold eye after she finished a duet with John. She came and sat by Stuart. She wanted me to understand she didn't hang around with other women. I wanted to say I wasn't a regular woman. In the dim blue light, everyone decided that I didn't have the experience to fit into the world of jazz, poker, and heavy drinking.

Dexter was sitting next to Helen. "You met Stu in the meetings?" he asked.

"Yes," I said.

"He's had a hard time getting there."

"I know."

"No," Dexter said, "you don't."

Helen and John were playing duets again. Stuart caught the beat. My second husband used to take me to jazz places in New York and said, "You don't want to nod your head or jerk your shoulder like that, no one does." I stayed very still, still as Dexter, who didn't move at all. When Dexter got up from the table, Stuart took his seat and put his arm around my chair. Helen was displeased.

Stuart invited everyone back to his house for chili, one of those foods men make, like spaghetti and barbecued steaks. His house was simple, neat, and straightforward. He would hate my house.

Helen set out the pottery bowls for chili. Was she expecting to stay with him? Would I be sharper to go now and see if he called me, or stay and stake my claim?

Jill clearly wasn't a stranger to Mehegan, who started a long rap about the House Un-American Activities Committee. He came in by talking about my stint with the British Embassy in D.C. at the time of the Army-McCarthy confrontation. Which leads, inevitably, to the Hollywood blacklisting—where Jill's

Hollywood background was revealed. This hits me with a thump. Dore Schary's daughter! Dore Schary, Oscar for *Boys Town* and head of MGM after L. B. Mayer. Jill was not only articulate, but show biz and politically aware.

She seemed startled when Mehegan turned the talk around to her father and defensive when it got down to the blacklisting. "People said he was a turncoat," Mehegan said. "The writers came to him for support and he took the studio's stand. That *is* what happened."

"I'm glad you were there to give a clear picture," she snapped. "My parents' families barely made it out of Russia during the pogroms, so my father was really wary of any Russian initiative. He was also involved enough in American politics to understand the power of the right wing." She had her explanation down by rote; she'd obviously rattled it off in discussions for years.

"He fought blacklisting, refused to name names, lost friendships with those who did, and because he kept his own job, he was able to help friends by hiring them under other names."

At this point, I stepped in on Jill's side. "Dore Schary was, if anything, patriotic to a fault, but at least he wasn't as eggheaded as those American Communists who turned a blind eye to Stalin. In fact, I had some leftist sympathies myself until I spent a little time behind the Iron Curtain as a journalist in Budapest, when Cardinal Mindszenty was in prison and taking pictures of police headquarters got you thrown in jail. All that made me realise that it had been an easy switch from a fascist alliance with Hitler to being a Stalinist bedfellow. Who wouldn't doubt the clearheadedness of American Communists?"

Jill smiled at my comments and, turning to me, changed the subject, "This is great chili."

We were laying out bits of our own lives, our ideas, and inclinations. The exchanges grew slower. Stuart's friends figured it was time to go. My heart was pounding. Stuart wanted me to stay behind. I saw it in his eyes, sharply focusing in on me behind the lens of his glasses. There would be that terrible silence, the awkward 'do you want some more coffee before you go?' all the while both of us knowing I wasn't going anywhere. How many times do you do this before you get it right?

Then Helen gave me a look over her shoulder as she left and said, "He's been through a rough time."

"I know that," I said. I really did. 'Don't hurt him,' she was telling me. Did I come across like the cool, privileged woman I'd fought so hard not to be? Could I have looked like that to anyone?

'Don't be careless with him' is what she meant. I couldn't have. I felt so careful, as if this were a brand-new exercise. I had to get each gesture, each word just right, such precision. Like every time I had fallen in love, it was exquisite—and excruciating. I was not going to do this again.

Two

When the band left, Jill hung around. We kept talking.

"I'll change the music," I said, "you've probably had enough jazz for tonight. Here's an old LP with two of my favorite concertos, Bartok's Third and Prokofiev's Third, by a wonderful pianist I met in London in the early fifties."

"I have a cousin who played in Europe then, a Brahms specialist, Julius Katchen."

"Jill, that's the guy on my Bartok and Prokofiev record!"

"So, you know my family already." Laughter.

"He used to stay with us in the summer and practice on my mother's Steinway," she said. "I had lessons myself, but hated practicing."

"My piano teacher was Albert Watson. Albert Finney would play him, with a limp and walking stick, a mass of flowing grey hair, and a permanent whiskey buzz. I quit after a half-dozen lessons, dissatisfied with my progress through Noël Coward's 'I'll See You Again,' and bothered by the shilling fee. Also, perhaps critically, I wasn't making any progress at seducing his daughter, who was gorgeous like a film star.

"Albert was of iconic proportions to me. At the war's end he was playing on weekend nights at the Working Men's Club in Pontefract. But back before the war, early thirties, he had been the master of the silver screen, the man who played the music for the 'silents' at the Alexandra, where my Great-Grandmother Cherryholme took me every weekday night."

"So, what were the first movies you remember?"

He was already wonderful to listen to. He sat back, reflective, eyeing me as he spoke. A true performer. His voice, manner, and the thoughtful blue eyes threw him back in time, put him somewhere in a world I'd never seen. This startled me. Had I ever seen a man whose life I couldn't rerun faster than he could? Was this my arrogance? Listen, I told myself, can you really *listen?*

"I thought the talkies were miraculous, *The Jazz Singer* was astounding, and John Boles in *The Desert Song* was larger than life, but music coming out of a picture is certainly not the same as music coming out of a piano six feet away. Just as a record of a brass band is miles away from the corpulent presence of a brass band, the puffed cheeks of it.

"There is reality and there is illusion, and there is a real illusion and an illusory illusion. I may be confused on this, but I think the difference is to do with witnessing the commitment, the real-time engagement with the creative act—the sweat of it, the joy and the pain. Perhaps this is why jazz truly *lives* in the nightclubs.

"I can remember watching and listening and, let's say, experiencing Bill Evans somewhere in the Village playing 'My Foolish

Heart,' and I felt the anguish in it and cried salty tears. Where have you been all these years? How long has this been going on? How long can this feeling be stretched out? Please stop; don't ever stop."

Yes, please, I thought, don't stop, don't ever stop.

"I'm writing a story for *Vogue* about love," I said. Was love the subject I really wanted to bring up? I added quickly, "I've just finished one about success," and I smiled. "It was largely to talk about my five cars, an L.A. thing."

"Not necessarily," he said. He looked me over so carefully.

He was such a new idea of a man to me. I'd had the different categories down pat. There were professional men with appropriate backgrounds, who'd want appropriate wives to maintain their families, their social worlds; artists, writers, professors, who wanted wives to maintain their security, like performers, who wanted wives to support their egos.

"A lot of Europeans have several cars," he was telling me, "one for the country, one for winters in the mountains, another for the city."

I had to tell him. "I've never been out of the United States," and suddenly what I've taken as a matter of course is embarrassing. "I was going to go with my best girlfriend one summer, but my father's back was bad, and I don't like to be far away from him when he isn't well. My mother wanted me to go, to see the things she'd never seen. Then when my parents finally went to Europe themselves, I was married. Ever since then, I've been working. That's an excuse. I guess the main thing is I'm not a city person. But I do love great rides, great cars, great roads."

"Then you're missing some of the great roads in the world," he said, with a slow half-grin. "There's nothing like a Jag on a great European road, winding through the Alps or speeding along the corniche from Eze to Monte Carlo. Maybe one day I'll take you." He lifted one eyebrow. "We'll have a Jaguar waiting at the airport and I'll drive you up through England to Yorkshire, across the moors to the North Sea."

"Perhaps," I said, almost in a whisper, "that sounds great."

I saw us standing on a cliff, looking out over the sea. I put a castle behind us. The wind was blowing in our hair.

"It was a nice thought," he said, feeling awkward, getting ahead of himself. We move on.

We sipped coffee, smoked, taking long drags, making the time go slow, sizing each other up carefully, thinking over the next thing we'd say here—to get it just right, as if our lives depended on it.

I told her I'd been working on a poem about love affairs called "The Best Times Were the Talking Times," and here we were talking about everything. Painting self-portraits for each other— Impressionist, even Pointillist, a dot or brush mark at a time, the image gradually taking shape. From 1964 Mustang convertibles to Buick Skylarks; from Christianity to Judaism; from *Lost Horizon* to *Wizard of Oz*; from *Finnegans Wake* to *Mrs. Dalloway*. From Here to Eternity.

The usual curriculum vitae material was dismissed in short order. Our mid-life range of experiences and self-examination brought us to focus on that tangle of values we sometimes dismiss as humanity and integrity. And the fact that we were both in a recovery fellowship was a great leveler.

I gave Jill glimpses of my childhood, my mother in a sanatorium and me living with my Great-Grandmother Cherryholme and my Grandma and Granddad Cawthorne in the town house opposite the Alexandra Cinema. Day after day with Edgar Rice Burroughs, H. G. Wells, Zane Grey. At night after, across the street with my great-grandmother to see the movies, often over and over again.

"There were endless quiet hours with no more movement than the pages of my library books and the dancing stars of dust above the window seat in the front room. Books were my pleasure every day. Even the new radio, with its music, talks, and plays seemed to be a second-rate distraction which demanded attention, rather than a story, which took me into it and allowed me to form my own images in my own time, and read, re-read, and re-read the best bits.

"I remember this part of my childhood as a time of great stillness and quiet; hours and hours of comfortable aloneness, serenity. An Edwardian soap opera with a handful of characters in entirely predictable and repetitive situations, beginning each morning with the trip to the henhouse in the back garden for the eggs to be boiled for breakfast with bread and butter fingers and a slice of toast with marmalade and a cup of tea.

"I loved our nightly trips to the cinema. Everything from the changing lights on the Austrian curtains before the films to the national anthem, when we stood to attention for the King and Queen. I suppose for multitudes of children all over the world in the 1930s, the movies were the ultimate escape, the ultimate promise of freedom and a better life. My love of books and cinema and my dream of America surely all came from these days with my old family. Probably, too, the sense I seem to have always had that life would be just fine for me."

"I had that same feeling," Jill said. "I used to sit in the big, empty living room, the bookshelves filled with a collection of classics. I'd pretend I was, maybe, Heidi, and all I ever had to do was read. I'd look out at the huge grey pine tree on the slope in our garden, and I was in the Alps."

I had imagined myself in every love story, watching from every window, waiting in every tower, or on the prow of every ship with his arms around me, or sitting behind him on every horse, my arms around him, my cloak flying out behind us. I have known you, I want to say, from the beginning of time.

As Stuart spoke about his first love, Danielle, he revealed the tender pale young man he'd been; earnest, eager to be with her, writing her poems, knowing he had nothing else to give and couldn't have found anything better to give anyway. Did he see something romantic about being Jewish? I told him I was Jewish, more because of what it meant to me, even as I ran away from it, than for anything it might mean to him.

"I don't want to talk about it, really, but you'll see, I do talk about it a lot," I said.

"I'm glad, at least you're assuming I'll be around to see that," he said.

We're trusting this attraction. So far there's no barrier. How captivating, like driving on a freeway with no speed limit.

"I never have to talk about being Jewish with Jewish men. We understand each other far too well. We can say things right out— what we hate about ourselves, love about ourselves, and can laugh about. Hip Christians like to do this with us, too."

"Am I a hip Christian?" he asked.

"Yes, probably," I said, "because we are having this conversation." There was a powerful connection here. We felt it.

"Would you like some ice cream?" he asked.

"Are you trying to say 'chill it'?" I laughed.

"Not exactly," he said.

I followed him to the kitchen. He was searching my face in this too bright light. We slid the ice cream off the ends of our spoons with the tips of our tongues, slowly, as you'd sip scotch, tasting each other's face in long, slow glances. Here we were, crazy about each other after what seemed like centuries apart.

"Only once since I fell in love with my children's father," I told him, "have I fallen in love with a Jewish man."

"Do you work at that?" he asked. "Do you avoid going out with them?"

"No, that would be too simple," I said, "and it's not exactly true. There were others, and I was crazy about them. We love to eat the same foods, we have the same kinds of relatives. I'd know every shoe he owns, every book he's read, the shows he's seen—he says 'show' instead of 'play'—what scares him (his mother), reassures him (his mother), what he loves best (his kids), drives him craziest (his kids). For me, if he's smart, sensitive, ambitious, and Jewish, I'll keep it simple, stay in love with my father and pick up sex on the side. It's amazing what a system you can work with years of good therapy." I looked at him, "Are you religious?"

Stuart thought about that. He knew the answer, of course. Was he thinking about what I'd want to hear? I don't think so. He rinsed the dishes, put them on the rack to dry, and faced me.

"I believe in a force for balance and order in the universe," he said, "and in that small shred of it called Stuart. That's my spiritual life, and I suppose what drives it is honesty. I was brought up with religion in the Church of England, and I sang in the church choir when I was a boy. But that's religion, not necessarily spirituality."

Looking at him standing there framed by the large window of dark sky, I could see his face as a child, so filled with promise.

"So, how did you begin to be a writer?" asked Jill.

"I was a sickly child."

"The tuberculosis?"

"Yes, and right after that a bad case of measles which left me with a 'lazy eye,' my right eye. So, at about age seven in primary school, a boys' school, I had to wear a black patch over my left eye to encourage the right eye to work harder."

"Oh, Stuart," said Jill, "you must have felt so isolated, so different, a bunch of boys staring at you, putting you down."

"Let's just say it made me very vulnerable. I think I resorted to storytelling as a defense against bullying. Who'd want to beat up the class's favorite storyteller?"

"Where did your stories come from?" asked Jill.

"Many of them were simply adaptations of stuff from boys' magazines—*Adventure, Skipper, Rover,* and so on—but I believe that I really absorbed some narrative skill from Mr. Taylor."

"Was he your schoolmaster?"

"No, better. Mr. Taylor was a lodger in my Great-Grandmother Cherryholme's house—a lodger, handyman. In truth, I believe he was Mary Cherryholme's lover, a 'fancy man,' as he'd have been called then. He was actually a bit larger than life. He'd started out as a sailor on sailing ships and worked his way up to captain of huge cargo boats sailing all over the world."

"So he told you his stories?" said Jill.

"Yes. He'd take me for long, long walks, which he said would be good for my breathing, and the miles would just slip by as he told adventure stories and travelogues. This probably also fed a desire to travel the world myself."

"You had a storytelling role model the same way I had in my father," said Jill.

"Exactly. At school whenever the teachers wanted a break, a quarter-hour or so, they'd ask the class who they'd choose to tell a story, and it was almost always me."

"That's the feel of the best books," said Jill, "when you're sure you can hear the writer's voice. That 'let me tell you a story' feeling."

"Yes. I'm still reminded of Mr. Taylor when I hear radio stories."

"Whatever happened to this wonderful man?" asked Jill.

"He died the year I won a scholarship to a grammar school. He left a fair amount of money, but some relatives who hadn't seen him for forty years showed up and claimed the inheritance he'd promised me for my education."

"But maybe the stories were his real legacy to you," said Jill.

"I can still remember how happy I'd be when we'd set out on the long, long walk," I said. "He'd put on his bowler hat, preen his white whiskers, button his jacket over the waistcoat, then reach in for his huge watch and say, 'Time to set sail, sailor.' And off we'd go. And when we were in the country, away from people, he'd burst into a sea-shanty and I'd join him in 'Down to Rio.'"

"Stuart, this is a great story," Jill said. "That was your writer's beginning."

"Then off to grammar school, where I began to write the stories down."

There was a part of me that had been yearning for this kind of conversation. Intelligent, broad ranging, mostly about the "arts" but without the pretension of so much book, film, picture, and music talk. We traded perceptions and experience, like baseball cards—'Oh, you've got a Mickey Mantle, too'—which engendered identifications of taste and preference.

Was I measuring Jill against the others, looking for green lights or red lights? My type, not my type, but I really didn't go for this nonsense about physical types. Love comes in many guises, but there might be correspondences. Perhaps each of us has an acceptable range of physical attributes in those for whom we fall. Once we get into the mind, heart, and spirit, it's much more tangled.

Jill was the most interesting woman I'd ever met. Perhaps it was her powerful combination of shrewd understanding of relationships with a streak of ingenuousness, all wrapped up in an eager curiosity. It was a palpable aphrodisiac.

It wasn't that I failed to notice her physical attractiveness. She had a provocative Shirley MacLaine look, with the short hair and bangs, a petite and beautifully rounded figure, glamorous green eyes, seductive breasts. And a sensational, broad, gleaming smile. But it was the spirit inside her that illuminated her, sent out rays, like that look she shot me in the diner that began all this. It's sometimes called personality, but that's a hackneyed description for this spirit that filled her with that wondrous and rare quality . . . INTERESTINGNESS.

This man was interesting, as interesting as the women friends I've loved, the friends whose long, smart phone calls make my heart pound. He was as varied in his conversation, as electric and deep in his emotional range, as utterly capable of talking about what he felt. Do you remember the line from *My Fair Lady*, "Why can't a woman be more like a man?" Easy to imagine how a *male* English professor could come up with such a concept. I often thought if only a man could be more like a woman, he could talk for hours, tell you of his longings, his dreams, ideas, and fears. He could be serious for an entire night. He hadn't told one football story, not once said, 'Did you hear the one about?'

But was this man too grand, too brilliant for me to touch, to sleep with? Would he be able to cut through my particular craziness, see it not as restraint but seductive challenge?

The intensity of this first night, the careful modeling of his words, the serious way he regarded every word I said, made it clear he was intrigued. There were men who could buy me new clothes, but not so many who had new things to say all night long. Was I leading him on because I thought he was compatible with my real priority of writing?

"I'm not what you think," I needed to tell him quickly, "I've had a rough story."

"I've heard that." He got up, came forward, and lit my cigarette.

"No, I don't imagine you've heard my whole, real story," I didn't look at him. "I've played around a lot. I'm not easy to be with. Mainly, the writing comes first—always has. I got into Stanford on a special writing pass. I wanted to be a real writer, not a screenwriter.

"Then, too, I caught this political fever from my father. I had one of the most popular call-in radio shows in L.A.—I love to talk; this was my favorite job. Then, real arrogant on speed, I refused to play commercials on the day Robert Kennedy was killed, so I was fired. I picked up my children, moved to New

York, and ran into real life as a journalist. To tell you the truth"—
I looked at him carefully—"I suppose I'm only at ease with
myself when I'm writing."

I have always thought of myself as a novelist, making up stories as I go along, but a journalist sounds more self-supporting.

"I know what you mean," he said carefully. He was pulling
aside a heavy curtain that had been there a long time. "I started
out to be a writer."

"I thought you were a journalist when I first saw you. You
don't look like a businessman." I said that too fast. "And you
don't sound like a businessman," I added.

"I'd imagined, when I emigrated to the United States, that my life
would be in writing, perhaps journalism, but after the
Washington Times-Herald's $32.50 per week, the offer of $400 a
month from Procter & Gamble was irresistible. So my wife and I
got on the train to Cincinnati and P&G, where my job, despite
being called management, was mostly about writing.

"I set the track records for promotion to Advertising Manager.
I took to executive life like a duck to water, and I loved working
with the advertising agency creative folk. But slowly I was
becoming dissatisfied with Procter & Gamble, as my increased
responsibilities became more financial than creative and my life
at home became increasingly unrewarding. I sought comfort in
booze and broads, and for quite a while that worked."

She winced when I said "booze and broads."

"I believe I crossed that invisible line into couldn't-care-less-
ness when my boss, Peter Link, and his wife, Liz, were in a plane
crash at the Greater Cincinnati Airport. I was the first to arrive at

the airport, then bribed my way into the morgue, but couldn't identify Peter or his wife. Then I came across my boss's body out in a corridor, still alive and recognizing me. He was cruelly burned all over. Somehow I was able to contact a doctor, and together we got him to the burn unit at a local hospital, where he survived for a couple of weeks.

"This was my boss, my drinking companion, my friend. He was a supporter of mine, and his death was a terrible loss. My drinking accelerated, and I lost all motivation.

"I became increasingly involved with other women and increasingly grandiose. I bought a huge mansion, scores of rooms, a swimming pool, ballroom, theatre, and acres and acres of land. But the house became a mausoleum, as I wandered from bar to bar wondering what the fuck had I done with my life. What had happened to the scholarship boy, the university young man, the Sword of Honour R.A.F. officer, the executive heading for the top?"

"Booze and broads," he said. It slipped out. Is he one of those guys my friends and I warn each other about? They can be well disguised—the English accent, the lyric quotes, the fine reflective expressions. Did I want to be involved with another alcoholic? I'd never been assured enough, confident enough, to fall in love with a man who was capable of changing his character, of seeing himself.

"My main thing," I told him, "was amphetamines, speed. My second husband told me the first time we met not to try to keep up with him. I was an inadequate alcoholic, couldn't hold enough to die directly. Only indirectly, say, in one of my car crashes." I was right away thinking about myself. Stop. Here was a man who really talked, so listen. "But didn't they send you to rehab?" I asked, looking him over.

"No. P&G was very conservative, WASPy and proper. At least on the surface." I pour us each another cup of coffee. "They didn't understand alcoholism and didn't want to. They wanted it concealed or out of town, like the hookers executives had on their out-of-state trips. So my 'creative excesses,' as they were called, couldn't be tolerated, and it was suggested I resign. I still have nightmares about it."

We drank the coffee, holding on to the cups, sipping, then gulping, with the exact rhythm I'd use with whiskey on a long night. "When Hefner was about to float Playboy Enterprises on the stock market, he felt the need for a blue chip manager to add to the executive team. No company in America was more blue chip than P&G, and I had my references, so he made me an offer I couldn't refuse. I was interested in the operation of Playboy, the company, which was impressive. But I didn't stay long at Playboy." I lit her cigarette. "It was a strange world I'd found myself in."

"So how did it end?" Jill asked.

"It never really began. I was the wrong guy in the wrong slot. Oddly enough, the house sex and booze didn't interest me, and I couldn't find a real rationale for my existence. I was living by myself on Lakeshore with Margaret back home cleaning up affairs in Cincinnati. Hanging out on Rush Street with guys like Ken Nordine, Mike Royko, and Jay Nash. In a strange, alcoholic way, I was feeling my way out of the business world back to the bohemian life of a two-fisted drinker and writer." This, I see, is more how Jill sees me. How will she see me as I keep changing?

"What happened to your wife, to your children?"

"Well, in a brilliant example of timing, I left Playboy the week my family moved to Chicago from Cincinnati. I figured, foolishly, I could make a living without much trouble."

"And did you?"

"Yeah, I got a lucrative consulting assignment from Pepsi in New York, and I was launched on to a consulting career. Until I met Zoe." I pause, tell myself this can wait. "I think we'll deal with that another time."

I wasn't sure I'd ever met a man who even went to Playboy. Worked there? I had a Bunny on my radio show. "I've kind of lived your story," I told him, "the other way around. You broke up your marriage in about the same way I broke up my first marriage, fueling lust with lots of chemicals and sharp propaganda. At first I thought it was all his fault. I had to get furious to leave, which made him angry and bitter, and that's never eased up. Later, I figured it had to be all my fault, that I'd destroyed his life, our children's. Then I realized we'd grown in different directions."

As I talked, Stuart brought me a fresh ashtray, as crystal-clear as I was trying to be. I wanted him to see how I really was. "Like a writer," I told him, "you can talk right through the night without setting pen to paper if there's another writer around to talk to. The air is alive with the spirits of characters left over from old books, like old ghost puppets, strings fluttering, waiting for us to pick them up."

He lit my cigarette. I touched his hand as he reached the heavy steel lighter to the cigarette, his hands steady as his mind. We were using writing to draw us close. What we were considering was love, but it was too soon to say that. So writing was the cover.

I had spent my whole life in love with a writer. That's who my father believed he was, laying the role of the producer, the executive. There was a different urgency about him when he was writing. He owned the excitement as a play came alive. Would it live, would it run? I could feel his longing as he'd wait for reviews, and his grief when the news wasn't good enough. I'd watched some of my writer friends who'd married writers, and some smart, balanced women who were not writers themselves. I'd seen how it goes. I would never marry a writer.

Writing is what she's all about. Writing is what I was all about until I forsook God for Mammon. We both love *talking* about writing, which is easier than actually sitting at a desk and picking up a pen. Yes, I'm sure we liked the way we looked, acted, spoke, got along, but we are soul mates because of the writing.

We talked until the birds sang, and the noises of a new day filtered through the sheer curtains.

"There's a meeting at ten-thirty at Saugatuck Congregational Church. How about it?"

"Of course," she said.

We parted at the church. No kisses or hugs. Friends watching us for clues.

"See you tonight."

"Sure, what time?"

"My place about eight, okay?"

"Yeah," she said.

Alone and apart. Such sweet sorrow and yet a warm, satisfied feeling. Not the post-prandial or post-sex satisfaction—a sort of exhaling—but an opportunity opening up feeling, almost like the liftoff of getting promoted. Perhaps Jill and I had pierced through to a core of conversational intimacy so intense that we'd passed the avenue marked SEX and advanced straight to GO. Perhaps my poem had been truly prescient . . . "The Best Times Were the Talking Times."

Suddenly, standing there alone in the church parking lot, I felt disconnected and unsteady. Does love make you dizzy?

Without help life is sometimes too much for us. I went to the beach and walked to the deserted end of it where I felt the frisson of spirits, perhaps the voices of my higher self.

"God, what am I to do? I feel I'm falling in love and I thought I was through with all that. What am I to do?"

The voice answered, "If you are through with love, you are through with life, and you are just beginning a new life. You must do the right thing."

"But what is the right thing?"

"It will be revealed."

"Why, when I try to turn over a problem to you, do you turn right around and hand it back to me?"

"Because it means you're ready to deal with it yourself."

"Does this mean I'll eventually have to deal with everything myself?"

"You've got it, son!"

"Here endeth today's colloquy with God," I said out loud. "Amen."

Be serious, I told myself. You're thrilled with these strong romantic feelings you're experiencing with Jill. You already believe that she's the love of your life, perhaps even your companion for the rest of your life, and yet it is oh so fast, this pell-mell rush of emotions, attachment. Isn't it like getting high and won't there be a downer soon after? Am I really ready for the responsibility? Can I honestly commit to this woman who has already been through so much? And how about her family and friends, and my family and friends? And can I genuinely support a married lifestyle? Hey! Hold on a minute! Marriage?!

Three

My younger son was making coffee when I got back to the house. Philip was a tall, handsome, blond, blue-eyed, very capable, self-starting twenty-something.

"I could hear you talking at some ungodly hour last night," Philip said. "You must know everything there is to know about each other." He shot me a sly look.

"No, Philip, we did not 'do sex' as you call it. She knows the outlines of my story, as I do hers."

He heard this was different. No joking. "You like her a lot."

"She's extremely talented and complicated. And a natural. As Pascal said, roughly, when we come across a natural style, we're always thrilled and delighted, for we expect to see an artist, and we find a human being."

"Heavy, Dad." He handed me a coffee. "I guess you really do like her a lot."

"Delightful. I guess what I'm really getting at, Phil, is that she is really a very intriguing woman. I think we'll talk again tonight."

"Great," Philip said. "See ya later, Dad. Don't take hostages."

He left, and now I began to worry about Philip and his relationship with his mother, who had not deserted him. And how would my other kids' loyalties be tested if there should be a new other woman in my life?

Jill came over the next night and brought daffodils. Philip and I were taping the new Freddie Hubbard album, *Super Blue,* and Jill seemed to like our father-son relationship. Perhaps she was weighing me up as a stepfather candidate for her two children I hadn't met yet.

Do I bring flowers? How many flowers was the issue, never mind discretion. Don't give him the idea you just snapped up a few from the garden. Does he have a vase?

When I arrived, he was working with his son on something. He had his sleeves rolled up. You could do this as an ad for an MGM father-comes-home movie. All you needed was Lassie watching.

His son Philip was also blond, but more delicate, reserved in a mannerly, not moody way. He was friendly, but needed no mother replacement. This was a different situation for me. I wanted a replacement for my children's father—not that I've exactly asked them if they wanted one, but I design everything. I saw this man was a mature father, neither competitive nor cute with his son.

There was another issue. Was his son here to chaperone? Was I here just for a visit, then I'd leave? Perhaps, I warned myself, I was to be an interesting friend. I was too interesting, of course, to lust after men who cared that I'll never get their laundry right. Yes, Philip had a friend over. They were going to the movies and then to hear music. Late, stay out late, please.

After Philip went out, I put on the original Getz and Byrd jazz samba album, the "Desafinado" cut. And here was Jill in my arms, and we were moving gently to the music. We kissed. Long, lingering movie-star kisses, over and over and over.

"Everything else between us seems just right," I said. "Perhaps we should see if the lovemaking part is as good as the conversation."

We went to bed. And we were suddenly teenage shy again.

"I don't like being without my clothes with the light on," Jill murmured. "Sorry about that."

"Why?" I asked.

"Not just you. Anybody. It's not how I look, it's the being looked at, explored, examined. I want to be the observer, not the observed."

"The star is not in charge—is it something like that?"

"Something." She clung to me. This has very little to do with traditional shyness.

"And I don't like sleeping without a light on," I said, "but we'll save the psychoanalysis for another time."

I compromised by keeping the light on in the hall. Jill borrowed a robe of mine, undressed in the bathroom, and slipped the robe off as she slid under the sheets. She didn't look at me either, and I saw her only briefly, silhouetted against the light.

I wanted to have this sex with him, if we could avoid the beginning part. This was what made you want to run, when you wanted the drink to get you through—the sound of other clothes rustling, unfastening, slipping off over bare skin. Would I look like what he had in mind? How long could I avoid facing him? After the undressing, there was the clasp, then the tender distancing for long, cool strokes. Thank God for the cigarette he had to snub out. French kisses need the smell of smoke.

Underneath, for me, it was chilly terror of all the road warnings, the alarms, the secrets I would never tell, which I get away with, because I write as if I'd tell it all on any talk show going by. That way no one ever really knows how private I really am.

So, what I seemed to have here was an appreciation of my secrecy, my reserve, the resolution that some nightmares must be kept tight to the chest, the tryout arena in my head where images whirled down the nightmare road of my sex collections. The reel ran through. Stay here. Well, yes. This was a surprise.

Getting this far, I knew I'd love him in bed. I knew he wouldn't laugh, tease, go fast, or go in for distracting games. Sensation filled the whole screen as he enveloped me in his strong, stocky form, his powerful arms, great muscular legs. He was a fortress of sexual stability. I could run the entire space, safe and wild as I can go. I could leap wide, high, shout and collapse and run again, and he was with me, catching every way I want to go. Thank God he's been around—around enough to shut up, to catch on fast. Cool and sultry all at once. This was perfection.

It was all so gentle, both of us very tentative, as though we were both straining not to sabotage this first encounter. As it was, the

tentativeness translated to tenderness and tenderness to arousal. My fingers were playing arpeggios over her silken skin, responding to the heat changes from the warmth of her loins and curving back to the cool of her shoulders. Then the trills on her moist parts and increasing power in the circling fingers, with some guidance from her hands, until the gasp of connection. And the little noises, oh yes, again the little noises, oh yes, and "now, now, oh yeah," and then the plunge, with the legs up and around me, the lips on her breasts, her erect nipples, and plunging as my peak came to follow on hers. Then hers a second time with my fingers and the moans, all the way to the shuddering sanctum and collapse.

Cigarettes and cups of tea. Jill asked, "Why do you have to have the light on at night?"

"I'm not sure. Possibly it dates back to the war, when we spent so much time in darkness. Remember the blackout, everything dark. And, of course, the air-raid shelters when the candles gave out."

"You must have been terrified."

"It was bad and it was good. With my dad away for about six years, I was the man of the house, but not really a man. I felt out of it because I was too young for the army."

He talked like a classic storyteller. I could tell already when he'd be about to begin, when he had a piece of life his memory had already composed. I curled myself around him, my head on the pillow, seeing with his voice pieces of his real life, not an old movie.

"That summer of 1945 was to have been a victory celebration, a rite of survival under skies as golden again as in those fancied, cloudless summers of childhood before the war.

"The war, the real war in Europe, we feared as we feared a neighborhood bully or a drunken collier on our way home from school, the struggle that took away our fathers, changed our mothers, and made us old before we had the chance to be young, finished in a frenzy of drink and dance, fighting and fornication around the Buttercross in Pontefract marketplace. From there, in the shadows of St. Giles' Church, the stalwarts of the King's Own Yorkshire Light Infantry band had blared the crowd through the gymnastics of 'Knees Up Mother Brown' and the sloppy sensuality of slow Glenn Miller foxtrots, into the final, shuffling stupor of 'Who's Taking You Home Tonight?'

"Our youth had disappeared in the flag-bunting-placard-and-broken-glass-littered morning in the wake of the Victory in Europe night, when we school lads staggered home by ourselves because the girls had slipped down alleys and into fields beyond with real men in soldier clothes."

"You're already writing that, aren't you?"

"Yes. I think I'll call it *Matthew Six:24*."

"Sounds like a code. That's wonderful."

"In a way it is, but it really refers to the chapter in the New Testament where we're told that we cannot serve God and Mammon."

"You've talked about balance," she said. "I read something once that a person writes or creates for three reasons: for the love of it, for the money, or for the fame. A balanced writer wants a piece of each. I go just for fame."

"I don't want to argue, but I think you're deeper than that."

"I am, but the fame thing is a deep, difficult longing. I'm a lot of trouble to be around," she warned me.

"Have I told you that I love you?" I said, looking directly at her. "Let me say it now, and again and again and again. I love you."

"And I'm afraid I love you—and I mean *afraid*. 'I love you,' for me, is always the beginning of a tough ending. Anybody can say, 'I love you.'" She was looking away from me.

"So let's turn all the lights out and make love again," I said.

She lay next to me, talking so honestly. "I never thought I'd fall in love again; not like this, raw, powerful, romantic."

I held her very close, and then I was struck with this primitive idea.

"Listen to me, Jill," I said in a strong voice, "we may not be married, but we are in love with each other, and Vikings take oaths that bind them together as close as any civil or religious ceremony or piece of paper. Maybe closer." I walked over to my desk and pick up my old fish-scaling knife. "We'll slit our wrists and mix our blood and swear an oath for each other."

"We will?" I was as absorbed in this game as a child of eight or ten would be. No one had loved me like this. This was such a strong, symbolic commitment. You don't mix blood and then forget to call the next morning. You don't cut your wrists and then think you're too much for each other. We were enough for each other. What a relief for everyone else.

"A fine madness called being passionately in love." I slit my wrist and blood oozed out in a thin red line. "I swear that for the rest of my life I shall love and protect you."

Jill was sobbing now, but the sounds were of relief, not hysteria. "I love you and trust you," she said. She held out her wrist. I nicked it with the knife, ever so gently, and waited until little droplets of blood oozed out.

"Let's hold the blood together," I said, and she responded, "I swear that for the rest of my life I shall love you and hear you."

We kissed, long, soft, hard, soft, our bodies clinging together. "We are soul mates," she said.

"With a blood oath to bind us forever," I whispered.

Then we made love, the love of wanderers seeking irrevocable companionship on life's voyage.

Falling in love. I've wondered . . . what does that mean? Was falling in love something you only do when you can't manage your own life? Like the rabbit in *Alice in Wonderland*—you let yourself go, you wander into it, trip, then plunge down, spinning deeper into another world. 'What can I do?' you say. 'I fell in love.' Who, these days, will fail to sympathize, or fail to envy? They'll turn it around, challenging my self-control, self-awareness. 'What are you doing?' friends will ask.

He was perfect. There was no question I wanted to be with him forever. How can I do this? Helen once coached me for an article, "Tell them never complain, be up for anything, smile whenever possible. Make him feel like a prince. Tell him he is *always* the best in bed."

Well, I'd made up my mind years before if he *wasn't* the best in bed, I wouldn't be there. This morning I woke up glowing, I felt lithe, easy. "You are a prince," I said, "and how do you like your coffee?"

Four

"Do you think your other kids will accept me the way Philip has?" Jill asked anxiously.

"I would guess so," I said, "but I'm more concerned about how Jeremy and Johanna will accept me, and I suppose we'll start to find out as soon as they arrive for lunch."

We're at my place in Southport, and Jill has bought a lovely selection of goodies from her favorite market.

"Don't expect our families to be the Brady Bunch," was the first sentence I heard from Johanna, who appeared at my place before her brother.

"Not a chance," I said, "but I hope it won't be the Hatfields and McCoys." Or, I think, the Montagues and the Capulets. I'm under no illusions about families and other people's children. They're quite capable of ruining a relationship.

Jill had forewarned me about Johanna. How she'd stayed with Jill after her parents' separation. How she'd been so badly let down when Jill's second husband, whom Johanna adored, left them. I instinctively liked what Johanna said, and I warmed immediately to this pretty, blue-eyed blond with a sharp wit. I saw her more as James Deanish than Brady Bunchish.

"I think you know my daughter, Susan," I said, "Susan Shaw. Pretty and blue-eyed, like you."

This seemed to be a good start, which was more than I could say for the first encounter with Johanna's brother, Jeremy.

"Hi, Mom," he said, bursting past me as he comes into the house. He was early twenties, tall and handsome, and worked in the mailroom at William Morris.

"Hi, Jeremy," I said, as he sat down in my chair at my desk, picked up the phone, leaned back to talk with his foot on the desk, twirling the phone cord in his left hand. "Come have some food."

The chatter around the table was innocuous enough, but I was jolted when Jeremy speared food with his fork from my plate. I got the message.

"Jeremy is all about control and territory," I told Jill after her kids rushed off to other pursuits. "I'm on his turf with you, and he'll defend his turf until he feels some trust in me, if he ever does."

"Understandable," replied Jill. "My kids have not had wonderful experiences with the men I've been with."

What I wasn't saying to Stuart is that deep down, Johanna was reflecting on her territory, our home, and this new man, the invader. She was going through phases I understood. When he came over to see us, dazed by what I see as rustic charm and what he saw as chaos, Johanna quickly handed Stuart a mug of coffee.

"You'll have to come for dinner. Mom said you make great chili, but we have the best spaghetti in America. And Caesar salad, but you aren't a salad guy, are you?" She laughed.

Johanna makes everyone feel like an old friend in five minutes. I heard her on the phone to her friend, "He got her home in time so she'd go with me to the doctor, *and* he got us there early. This has never happened before." I could tell she was accepting him when she joined forces with Stuart against me, like buddies. "Cars are a big problem for my mother," she said to Stuart, "but I always have the car that's running."

In the early days, when each hour together was dense with information or still with heavy wonder, Stuart and I spent hours driving the winding Connecticut roads, picking up images, places, that will cement this construction we're putting together here. Dr. Mike's ice cream store out in Bethel becomes "where we go" by the third time we stop there. And on these rides, where no one could get to us then, we dig deeper, we learn more. We talked a lot about the kids.

"There's no instant or magic answer," he said. "We just have to try to be as supportive as we know how with our five kids. After all, they aren't children anymore."

He's telling this to me, over and over. "The most important thing," he said, "is we'll deal with each one on that individual's terms."

The more we talked about our children, I wondered whether Jill still saw hers as children rather than young adults. I also realized how we bring our own singular perspectives to the topic of age and responsibility. A voice inside me said, 'But Stuart, by the time you were their age you'd been through a world war, taken care of a family,' and so on and so on.

Jill said, "Do you really think your kids want to deal with someone else? Do you want to deal with my kids? Do we even want to consider that?"

"I don't know how good I can be at this, but I do know that if there's going to be a lasting thing between us, it will have to include the children." As I said this, I was becoming conscious of what was really going on here. We were moving toward commitment, and both of us knew intuitively that the commitment went well beyond the fine, careless rapture of a man and a woman. There was a commitment to the connections, the relationships, all the paraphernalia of each other's lives.

Five

When we fall in love again we still carry the baggage of the old relationships. It's not a good idea to store this baggage away from view. Better to haul it out and reveal it for what it is. As some wise person once said, "You're only as sick as your secrets." This was what was going through my mind as I lay next to Jill after a night at my place.

I'd been thinking about my first wife, Margaret. More specifically and critically, I'd been thinking about a dilemma I now faced. Weeks before I met Jill, I'd invited Maggie to Southport for a week's holiday. She'd had some surgery, which I suspected was quite traumatic. I thought she'd enjoy being near some friends in the East, our son Philip, theatre in New York, and so on. Nothing romantic. No revival meeting. I knew it might be trouble with Jill, who could easily jump to the wrong conclusion, especially with Margaret sleeping under the same roof. And particularly with Margaret arriving only a few days after we'd taken a blood oath to each other.

"How do I handle this?" I asked my mentor, Trenton.

"Simple," he said, as usual. "You tell it to her exactly as you told it to me—straight out. The tough part is the timing."

"What do I do about that?" I asked.

"Simple. Pick a time when her confidence and trust in you is at a high point, a time when you're demonstrating your forthrightness."

"Okay, Trenton. I'll try."

"Attaboy. You'll get through it."

I woke up in his house. It was six in the morning. He turned and reached for me. I slipped out of bed, wrapped on a robe he'd put at the end of the bed, and brought some coffee in for him. He leaned over the edge of the bed to reach the mug and took a sip of coffee. I tossed off the robe and slid back in bed. He reached over and touched my bare shoulder.

"I was up around five this morning," he said, "and when I came back to bed you were still sound asleep. I stroked your skin, your body so warm and soft under the blanket, and cool on your shoulder above the covers. I loved touching your skin, feeling the change of temperature."

Having him say he was looking at me like that, touching me while I was sleeping, that's what all the perfume and flowers are supposed to say.

We spent most of the morning in bed at his house. Erotic lounging, a novel approach to morning. Was it European? I had one man who would flick through the sports channels, news channels, weather reports, then call his running partner because he might be a minute late. He'd grab his coffee and dash out in full gear. I learned not to have lunch with such a man; he'd know so fast that I'm not his idea of a woman. However, Stuart, I could see, had always been into romantic adventure. Some of my friends will think, 'Here we go again', and some of his friends would not suggest me for him.

Now, I couldn't take myself away from Stuart, even though I was away from my work, my kids, my kitchen. Love puts you in a kind of isolation.

Just as he turned off the shower, I heard the doorbell ring. I stayed silent in bed, as if I were sound asleep. I saw him dash past the bedroom door with a towel around him to open the front door.

"Hello, Peggy." Yes, one of his romantic adventures. "I guess this is not a good time," she said. Can you hear the withering look?

"Not exactly."

"Well then, I'll just come in for a few minutes," and I imagined her pushing past him because they were now in the hall. "Why haven't you been calling me?"

"Peggy." He cleared his throat and started again. "As long as I have known you, I haven't been in the habit of calling unless I have a specific date to arrange."

You'd think she'd see him standing there in a towel, slap him, and just go. Would I? She was hanging on, making it worse. "Something's different. Something's wrong here," she said.

"Peggy" he said, "listen. This isn't a good time to do it, but you should know I have fallen in love with someone else."

"So that's that?" she asked.

"That's that," he said.

She left, and he came back to bed. Did I feel like a winner or a nervous compatriot?

"Look," he said, "I promised her nothing except occasional companionship. She wrote her own script, but she did behave with remarkably good taste. At least I was honest." He sighed.

"Yes, you were that."

"I hope we can both be that honest about everything, Jill," I said.

My conversation with Trenton about Margaret's visit came charging back into my head. Yes, yes. This was the time when Jill saw me dealing honestly with the past. This was the time to tell her about Margaret's visit.

"And one of those everythings is about my ex-wife, Margaret. You have to know that we still have a relationship, which is amazing, considering the terrible times I gave her when I was into the booze and playing around with other women. She's a great woman, terrific mother, and we are, after all, the parents of three kids."

"I think that's very civilized of you both," said Jill. "I couldn't do that. I don't have any kind of relationship with my children's father."

I could feel the tension rise. "Well, that's how it is." I sat down on the edge of the bed next to her. "Jill, this may be a hard part for you, but before we met, I'd invited Margaret up to spend a week with me."

"You mean in Southport?" Jill asked.

"Yes," I said. She seemed to be taking this in slowly.

"And when is she coming?"

"In a week."

"And where is she staying?"

"Here, in my house."

"Not here, not in your house," Jill said. She looked at the bed.

"Yes, she'll be staying here in this house with me. I'm truly sorry about this, but it's a commitment I made weeks ago, and I want to honor it."

"I don't know what to say." She pulled her hand away. "I don't know how I'll deal with that, you being together. I don't know if I can deal with that." She stood up. "I think I'll just go now."

The last time I'd called Margaret to talk about the kids was when I asked her to come up to visit. I must have been troubled enough to talk to my sponsor. Did this mean I was unsure of what might happen when Margaret was next to me? Was there anything sexually between us? Would there be any temptation to start all over again, particularly now that I was sober? Did Margaret have any fears or expectations?

In short, was I being bloody stupid, putting temptation in my way? No, I thought, even before talking to Trenton. I'm no longer the immoral SOB I used to be, and I have too much respect for Margaret to screw up the situation. It was also paradoxical that I've loved Margaret and cared for her, and yet I constantly betrayed her. Surely the best amends I could make to Margaret would be to show I could behave in a caring and decent way while she was here.

"Of course his sponsor will tell him it's a great idea. And, of course, she'll get him to come back to her," I'm crying on the phone to my friend Holly, "so I can just forget the whole thing. But maybe she'll smell my perfume on his pillows and leave."

"Someone else's perfume won't astonish her," Holly said. "This is where you're testing your trust in him. And maybe he's testing his commitment to you."

If he had any fears, he'd cancel her visit. Men never know what fears they should have until it's too late.

When Margaret actually arrived in Southport, Jill broke down or, rather, flared up. "But you'll end up sleeping together, and you'll fall for each other again now that you're sober," she cried.

"Jill, don't be an idiot. Our marriage is well and truly over, and we simply care for each other and our children. You know, I did spend twenty years married to this woman, and I gave her a lot of hell right from the start."

"So, I won't see you for a whole week," she said. "I can't deal with that, Stuart."

"Jill, it's not a whole week. We've just started this early-bird meeting every day at seven-thirty A.M. We can see each other every morning and have coffee afterward. It won't be so bad."

"I'm still worried about it," she said.

"Yes, and so am I. I'm worried about you being worried, because that in essence says you can't trust me—which plays into your basic fears of abandonment. Listen, there's not going to be any hanky-panky with Margaret, no sex orgies, nothing. Just plain old friendship and a shared interest in our kids. In fact, the first thing Maggie said to me was, 'I just want to lounge around and not interfere with your recovery or whatever you're into.'"

"I have work to do anyway," Jill sniffed, "and the kids and I can have a lot of people over."

"I'm afraid Stuart's housekeeper is probably only too thrilled to get the house exactly the way she imagines his wife will like it, spraying away any hint of my perfume, hiding my cigarettes. At least Margaret, this woman, has some formal place here and isn't an unconnected interloper." I was glad I was seeing my therapist, Gloria, today.

"I told Stuart I won't see him until his wife has left," I said. "He told me I could use the time to write, reminded me of my deadline. But I just snapped at him that maybe he wasn't really over his wife."

"That's not the problem," Gloria said, "although it would help if you would stop referring to Margaret as his wife. Are you putting yourself down here?"

I watched her as she twisted around with a glance at her notes. "Is he a con artist?" she asked.

"You're asking me the question I don't dare ask myself," I said. "I want to trust him. I know his wife —Margaret—his 'ex-wife'— okay?—is only here because she's been sick and he promised her a trip here. He keeps his promises—he's a good man. Margaret still likes him enough to be with him, and he honors her enough to care for her. No, he's no con artist." I am completely clear on that. "But I'm still jealous of anyone who has one second near him."

As Margaret's visit unfolded, I filled up with emotions centering on how badly I had behaved with Margaret, the lies, the cheating, the terrible embarrassments, the pain and the suffering. Part of me wanted badly to stand in the dock and recite chapter and verse of all my transgressions, betrayals, sins, and somehow atone for them, make amends. But if amends are designed to heal and not to injure, I came to the conclusion that a full-scale mea culpa could only be harmful and open up old wounds.

Nostalgia swept up in me on occasion, especially when Margaret tuned into good times we had had.

"You used to say on drives like this, 'How I envy the road that has somewhere to go.' Remember?" Margaret is in the front seat next to me, driving back from a play in Manhattan to my place in Southport. A cloud-dappled moon peers over the parkway and stars are sequinned into a navy-blue sky.

"Yes, I think it came out of a poem, perhaps one of my own," I said. "I'm not sure. But I've always liked the freedom in those words—if you can just get out on the road, go anywhere, be anyone."

"Maybe it's your Viking heritage," Margaret said, "because so much of your poetry talks about travel and voyages."

"There was a lot of adolescent intoxication with mythology, and a left-wing bias I guess."

"Youthful," said Margaret, "but your poetry was still very good, and I remember how happy we were when your first poem was published in America."

"What I am remembering now is a night drive like this, aeons ago. We'd been staying with the Gelbs at Lueza's family place in the Adirondacks. A wonderful, wonderful holiday with a great signature tune, Elvis's 'All Shook Up.' Now it's the drive back to Cincinnati I'm thinking of, about twenty-four hours, stopping only for gas, and most of it at night on two-lane highways because the interstate only went as far as Buffalo, leaving that long, long last stretch down through Ohio from Cleveland to Cincinnati."

"You were having hallucinations by the time we hit Columbus," said Margaret.

"But I did feel that wonderful sense of freedom. I was actually living a road movie; I *was* the Beat Generation. I could see

Coltrane and Mingus and Monk in the headlights, blowing the wheel of the Packard—called Bessie after big, fat mama Bessie Smith—and the foot pedals my bass drum. Jam session journey; roadway riffs. I had somewhere to go and it was a seductive nowhere."

"Sorry to get in the way of your riff," Margaret said, "but do you remember how that thousand-mile epic ended?"

"No, tell me."

"Well, we'd reached Norwood, a piece of Cincinnati about a mile from home, when we lost the transmission on the Packard. To complicate life, it happened as we were straddling a railroad track, and a train—ever so slowly—was coming toward us. How you got us off that track all by your own pushing, I'll never know. But we made it."

Yes, I thought, we made it then because of her. What was missing in the relationship was missing in me.

After we got home and just before we adjourned to our separate bedrooms, I took Maggie in my arms and said, "I'm really sorry for all the hurt I caused you. I wish I could undo it all, but all I can do is to say I'm sorry. I loved you very much, and I still do."

"I love you, too," she said, "and it can't all have been one-sided, so let's leave it all alone."

"Thank you, Maggie."

"Good night, Stu."

The next night I decided I would have to spend with Jill.

Stuart was having dinner with Margaret that night, her last night. No matter what he said, he's close to Margaret's cultured voice, her familiar elegance, and it will be all over with me. She's not all wrapped up in work, and the children she's absorbed in are *his* children.

I had fallen half asleep around two in the morning when the phone rang. "Can I come see you?"

"Please," I said. Do not sound desperate, just eager.

I let him in, he slipped in beside me, and the log bed creaked as I twisted away. I punched my anger into the pillows. So, he could leave his wife one place, and just come here, my place, any time. Had he told Margaret we are this close, get her to see how needy I am? Would she be sympathetic? I doubted that. Stop it, I told myself, grow up. Maybe this is the way to keep us together, to keep our passion fierce and strong. I turned to him, desperate, and I couldn't resist.

Now, he had his arm around me, his profile lit by the moon shining down through the skylight. "We seem to have reached the point where it is possible to spend time apart without your feeling insecure," he said.

"Does this mean we aren't afraid the other one will be doing something absurd?" I said.

He didn't catch the edge in my voice. "Perhaps, more importantly, there is a growing feeling that if one of us wants to be alone, it is simply because one wants to be alone, to do things or think about things, without worrying that the separation has anything to do with rejection. Indeed, our time alone may be constructive. Before I went to sleep last night, I reread some pages of Graham Greene's novel, *The End of the Affair*. I have a new awareness that this book, written in the first person, is Graham Greene's own story of a love affair in his later years."

"Am I a love affair of your later years?" I slipped in a question.

"You're the love affair of my life," he said. He tried to keep the conversation about our writing, not our relationship. Was this so I didn't sidle it over to questions about Margaret? They simmer here; turn down the burner, I told myself. He caught the heat. "Do women always want to talk about the relationship? How long before you will be secure enough so you don't have to worry about it every day?"

Only when your wife is here, I thought. Don't do this. I stopped myself. "But then you'll think I'm taking you for granted," I said.

"No, I won't," he said, "but we're talking about Greene's book. Can I go on? I'm especially interested in this book because it deals with the main character, himself, as a professional writer. A lot of it makes sense to me. He says, for example, that he does not have a gift for describing people except through their actions. I identify with that since I have little interest in detailed descriptions except where physical characteristics or mannerisms are related to the action or story."

"So would you like to explain why I'm wearing your black velvet robe, then?" I asked.

"Because you're worried that I won't remember how sexy you are," he said. "You're afraid because of Margaret, which I understand. I don't want anyone else close to you, either."

"Seeing you here, now," I said, "I'd say that having you, loving you is the point of my days. You give me all the light and life." I threw my body around him, "You're everything."

I wondered now as I watched Stuart lying here beside me, tracing the structure of his face, will you be my fortress, protecting me against invaders? Does he know there will be days when I'll pound against the fortress, screaming to get out? Does he know he will also need me as his sheltering fortress, my busty silence around him?

Anna Kavan began *The Visit*, "One hot night a leopard came into my room and lay down on the bed beside me." This one here traps me in bed with feelings I will not name. Is he one more dangerous passion that will tear me to shreds? Trapped by his refreshing, archaic, romantic declarations, I'm not going anywhere. At the same time, I'm going everywhere I've never been.

This was the night the log frame bed finally came apart and we slept on the floor.

We somehow survived the Margaret interlude. I had had mixed feelings about telling Margaret of falling in love with Jill, but I was pleased that I'd kept that out of our talks while she was with me in Connecticut. A month or so later, I decided to bring Jill into the open and called Margaret to tell her about the new situation.

"You have my best wishes," said Margaret, "and I'm especially pleased that you both share the same spiritual program, so you'll keep on the straight and narrow."

"Absolutely critical," I agreed, "and thank you for understanding that."

"Well, good luck again."

Margaret, indeed, gave me a great gift in the week we spent together. She never once made me feel guilty about the wrongs I had done her. She applauded my venture into sobriety. I will never forget the feelings of kinship and support this attitude of hers engendered.

So, not only did Margaret have a pleasant break with me in Southport, but the experience was the first acid test of Jill's ability to trust me in a provocative situation, which strengthened our faith in each other.

Six

Stuart hates shopping. My kind of shopping, where you cruise places, talk to everyone, and decide what you want when you get there. Hayday was open late tonight. We're shopping for the July Fourth party, picking up warm pies, ripe peaches, and pudgy chickens. This is not Stuart's sort of place. He likes big brands, big-aisled supermarkets. He wants to go in, get what he needs, and leave.

Farmer's bread, yes, with rosemary, and another one with olives. Lots of fresh-squeezed orange juice. I'll put masses of fresh peas in the salad of baby potatoes.

"What's your favorite salad?" I beamed at Stuart.

"I don't really care for salad. Caesar, I guess."

"The apple pies are over there, we'll need four," I said. "I'll do a risotto salad, creamy, wonderful with a lot of thyme. Most people just don't use enough spices or herbs. It's like making love; you just have to put in more than you'd guess could be possible."

"You're trying to get my attention," he said. "Don't think I'll confuse food and sex for a moment."

"Unless it's dinner just for you." I dropped shallots into a paper bag.

"Something like that," he said. "Don't you have enough flowers?"

"Never," I said, my arms wrapped around zinnias, daisies, and tiny branches of ultramarine periwinkles. "I have to get some more cheese." I handed him the flowers. "I'll be right back."

Stuart looked at his watch.

Just because Jill and I had fallen in love did not mean that friends and relations fell in love with the notion of our falling in love. Nor did it mean that we were immediately enamoured by each other's entourage. The balance of power shifted, or was it the balance of terror? There certainly followed a period of adjustment with varying degrees of pain and, hopefully, some gain.

I advised all my young friends about this potential quagmire. "Expect all your relationships to be redefined, and decide what your priorities are." Some friends you may keep, but invariably you'll lose some, and even the nature of the friendships you retain will change and must be carefully tended.

In some ways, this was a beneficial condition for me because I'd stopped drinking and largely given up on my drinking buddies, and most of Jill's friends didn't appear to be heavy drinkers.

It was July Fourth and, fittingly, I sensed a threatening loss of independence on this day when Jill threw a party at her house. The party highlighted some differences between us that hadn't emerged in our brief times together.

I was laying out blue-and-white-checked tablecloths. Stuart glared around the room. He has not been easy on my house. "It may be a kind of decorator's dream" (not any decorator *he'd* know), "but it's completely unworkable," he said, surveying the big, open room that serves as kitchen, dining and living room. "There are no places for groups to form and talk." He'd, of course, dated divorced women studying interior design.

"So move some chairs," I told him. "It's not formal, just put things where you want."

Today, he was cool to people he didn't know and irritable with my kids' friends. His guy friends stood in a corner looking awkward. All men have friends called "guys" or "buddies" who are not going to be crazy about you. If they're married, you'd be nice to the wives, but you won't like each other. There was no point in discussing this. After two marriages and other serious situations, I'd learned, sort of, to keep quiet about things you can't change much.

"What you really want is to go," I said. We stood looking at each other. "You can."

"There's too much going on at cross-purposes." He looked down; his hair fell across his forehead. "Definitely unbalancing." Now he looked back at me, threw out the large chest. "I have a protective feeling about you, and I resent people getting at you, using you and your place."

"You're talking about *your* resentments," I snapped, "they aren't mine, and I have never had a decorator who talks about space units. You're being this way because you got stuck talking to one of my friends, and she didn't light up to you. She's scared for me—like you are—only you're what scares her. Do you want another hamburger?"

The party was like a river of people that inexorably splits into tributaries with singular identities: Jill's people, girlfriends; my people, guy friends; Jill's two children and their friends. Each tributary had its own character, and all these tributaries shared one common characteristic—suspicion and distrust of the others. Each group in its own manner seemed to be signaling, 'Hey, this person, Jill or Stuart, is my person. I don't want this person hurt, and I don't want to surrender my piece of this person.'

These territorial manifestations came in various guises, from the seemingly friendly, 'Jill doesn't really like sporting events of any kind, she's more a party girl,' to the overtly hostile, 'Gosh, I hope you don't take Stuart away from our jazz sessions.' And if all the kids could have spoken with one voice, it would probably have said, 'Please guys, don't take away our weekend party house and crash pad!'

The July Fourth party made me quite dizzy, not with the eddying crowd and the music and the chatter, but with the waves of partisan emotions washing relentlessly over us like North Sea tides.

"It's been a vigorous Fourth," Stuart said. "It's a relief it's almost over."

"Is it really? Only because you are not glaring at me."

"You may have been sober much longer than I have, but you are really screwed up in your relationships with your kids, your friends, people you work with—and I *know* this is going to be trouble."

"That's how you see it," I shouted. "You're different. I don't do life the way you do, and don't want to!"

"This may sound brutal," his voice dropped even lower than usual and darkened, "and there's no question that I love you, but I simply will not deal with all the shit around you. You're being used on every front, and if you won't see it, then maybe we'll have to have some kind of separate life."

I was crying, terrified inside. I remembered hearing my parents shouting in their bathroom after my grandmother, my father's mother, moved in with us, 'You have to decide! One of us has to go.' How do you make that decision?

He took both my hands quietly, "Jill, listen, you're upset, because you want me to be a part of all that you are, all that you have, but I sense very strongly that a lot of that is *definitely* not good for me, and may well not be good for you."

"So, unless I make some changes it's over," I said.

"I can't tell you what to do with your life. I'm not in the business of reorganizing your life."

"But you're exactly in that business! You're brilliant at reorganizing entire companies. Of course you'll come into my life with that perspective: change this, fire this one, cut this out. We are different. What's not good for you may be what I need."

I didn't want to tell him what he probably knows already. What I need most of all is the order and freedom to work. So he may have exactly the answers I need.

"So, I may have to make some hard choices," I said.

"You know in most situations what it is you have to do," he said, "and the hard part is when there isn't any choice."

We were both trying not to talk about how we could never live together if this was how I lived.

While I was saying this, I actually felt that, despite her sobriety and long-term therapy, Jill had really screwed up relationships with her folks, her kids, and her friends. They all seemed to be taking from her. Was this going to be trouble or was I wrong? Was I being the overpossessive lover?

"Look," I added, "I'll try to be as friendly and diplomatic as possible, but I'm going to insist on some separation from these connections of yours, some independence for the two of us."

Jill was obviously thrown by all of this, but we kept calm, left the house to her kids and their friends, and headed back to a quiet interlude in bed at my house.

Seven

"I really feel," I told Jill a couple of weeks later, "that we should aim for a smooth relationship with our parents."

"You mean *my* parents," she said. "Your parents live in England. Your relationship with them *is* smooth and orderly, distant, just the way you want."

"True," I said. "Still, we'll need all the support we can get. Let's go into New York and take your parents out for lunch, okay?" Jill saw very little of her parents, even though they lived only an hour away in Manhattan.

"Okay. Sure. Soon," she said, and I sensed in the note of reluctance in her tone of voice that there was something amiss with the relationship.

"Is there something wrong with that?" I asked.

"Well, they're not really that well, physically I mean."

"All the more reason to go see them," I responded.

"I suppose so, but they're probably having a hard time."

"Perhaps I can cheer them up." I suspected that Jill might be having a hard time dealing with her father's fall from power since his glory days running MGM. For obvious reasons, if this were true, my own identification with this loss of power might be useful, accepting.

At last Jill agreed to drive into Manhattan to have lunch with her parents. A lovely day for a drive into Manhattan's West Side. I dropped Jill off to visit Gloria, her long-time therapist. I parked the car and wandered over to Lincoln Center. Nureyev had a return engagement with the Joffrey Ballet in a program billed "Homage to Diaghilev." This was a year for Diaghilev nostalgia.

I'd been several times this spring to the Met's Ballet Russes costume exhibit and was intoxicated with it. Somehow the old magic was conjured up in the static exhibit, darkly lit like a theatre during performance, the costumed mannequins like dancers in repose. Moving lights picked out this figure and that, giving a feeling of motion. The music of Stravinsky, Debussy, Ravel, and Tchaikovsky sang the vibrancy of the theatre into the exhibition rooms.

It all swept me back to my college days and my introduction to Sadlers Wells, my crush on Ninette de Valois, and my passion for Svetlana Beriosova. Such days and nights, with music on an old-fashioned record player with thorn needles and a huge horn.

I reserved two orchestra stalls seats for Nureyev and the Joffrey, then strolled across to Central Park to kill time before I met up with Jill and her parents. Tuesday afternoon in the park with Stuart.

A flower-bedecked, dismal horse and decrepit carriage rumbled by with a woman and young girl in it full of smiles like more flowers. Two cyclists swooped by, one with a huge stereo on his back. Roller skaters glided by, stealth skaters, like World War II planes.

Curtain time. Over to the Café des Artistes, where I had a

Perrier at the bar. The hostess advised me that a lady awaited me at a table by a window, and I joined a radiant Jill. We held hands for a few moments before Mr. and Mrs. Schary arrived.

Mrs. Schary—Miriam—was slight with a beautiful, pale complexion. She had blond hair that was surely a wig, and was wearing a simple pink dress. Miriam was wearing shades and had a slight paralysis on one side of her face. For no reason whatsoever, I liked her immediately (did she resemble Margaret years ago?), definitely upmarket and artistic.

Mr. Schary—Dore—was formal, erect, dark blue suit, striped shirt and conservative tie. He wore steel-rimmed spectacles, which suggested 'don't mess with my head.' Dore and I plunged right away into words, into books. His autobiography, *Heyday,* was at the galley stage. Miriam said she read a couple of paragraphs, then cried for ages.

Later I said to Jill, "Is this what keeps you away from your mother? The despair over the glory days when Dore was king of MGM, and she was his consort?"

"Maybe," said Jill, "and the fear about appearance. My mother never accepted her face. Don't forget that Hollywood was all about looks. Think of an Oscar night crowd and how conventionally beautiful everyone looks. I had bad acne as a teenager, and I knew how she felt. We couldn't bear each other's discomfort, but at the same time it bound us together. She felt she would have been a really great pianist, but she couldn't bear being on stage, being stared at."

"But I've seen her paintings at your house," I said, "and it's clear she picked up great classical technique. She's a talented artist."

"Yes, but she's bitter. And she's riddled with arthritis, which is why her hand shakes holding her glass of Perrier."

"Well, I didn't sense bitterness," I said. "As for the shakes, I wondered whether she drank and was in withdrawal."

"She does drink," said Jill, then added quickly, "but I think it's mostly arthritis."

"That explains even more so her despair as an artist," I said.

"Think how terrible it must be not to be able to use her talent with any assurance," Jill said. "I think that's what hurts the most—she barely paints at all anymore."

Stuart called my father "Mr. Schary" and my father was captivated. They talked about words, the definitions, origins, and misuse, which they found particularly engaging. Stuart saw that my father could be warm and perceptive. I felt I had brought my father a gift.

My mother roused herself into an alluring, if ravaged, presentation. The best of the antique gold cigarette holders perched on her forefinger, clamping the cigarette so the smoke veils the face she hates. The holder was Marlene Dietrich's idea, she tells Stuart. Sometimes it was Gloria Swanson's idea.

"I think," I told Jill later, "that your dad was assessing my politics. He had a keen response when I talked about writers working for the WPA in the Roosevelt era. He was quick to point out that a few years later those same writers were being blacklisted and denounced as Communists."

"They liked you a lot," Jill said. "Daddy especially liked that you're a generous tipper."

"Perceptive," I rejoined, "but I'd like to be thought of more seriously than a big spender. And you're unfair about your mother. I don't know how you can hate her. She's so adoring of you, so genuinely loving."

"It's too unbearable," Jill said. "I cringe, I die to talk about her, to think about how she's collapsed. We can't bear watching idolized parents grow old. It's like watching what will happen to us. There is no appealing way to look at it. My father is so tragic, missing his former power."

"You don't see it well at all," I said. "*You* miss what he once had, but he's got a far more interesting and deeper influence in the world he's moving in now. Perhaps what *he* misses is his physical strength and the illusion that life will somehow go on forever. I think that's what you really can't bear. Your mother's thoughts may seem disjointed, but they actually are quite insightful. She simply has a different perspective and can't be bothered with ordinary chatter."

Eight

"Jim and Jane Holden are two of my oldest friends," I said to Jill, "and they're really anxious to meet you. They suggest dinner at their house on Saturday night."

Jill flashed that harried, hunted look she gets when stressed. "So they knew Margaret," she said, "and they'll be comparing me to her and wondering how come you're with a hippie writer."

"Oh sure," I said, "and they'll vote against you and our whole affair will be off. As a matter of fact, I'm sure Jane will be wild about you. She knows from her own experience what it's like to have a failed marriage and a child before she found the love of her life with Jim. And, besides—you'll love this—she's been fixing me up with dates for months. So you can tell she has my best interests at heart and is certainly not fixated on Margaret."

"So what shall I wear? I can put together a lady outfit, maybe get a quiet little dress, understated elegance?"

"Look, Jill, Jane and Jim are very down-home people and

wonderful friends. You could wear a T-shirt and jeans if you wanted, but I'd suggest something a bit theatrical."

Jim was in one of P&G's New York ad agencies at the same time I was with P&G in Cincinnati. Like most of us young executives in those days, Jim was not your basic business school suit. He came from St. Louis and was a genuine show-me guy. He was smart, industrious, highly disciplined. Jane was a New York girl, making a career for herself in public relations—very bright, very attractive, very sociable. She'd had a bad marriage and was working to bring up a young child. When they became engaged, I threw a party for them. All of us felt that this was a match made in heaven between a tremendously desirable woman and a very eligible, macho bachelor.

That, of course, was years ago. Jim had built a powerful career for himself in the media business. They now lived in a beautiful old house in Greenwich, Riverside. They had one daughter from this marriage.

Jill dressed in an absolutely fabulous Kamali outfit and looked quite wonderful. As she launched into her Hollywood stories, I got a full appreciation of how good she was in these social settings. A true performer.

Jane probably ran the kind of house Stuart would love and need. She'd be the kind of hostess who had everything organized a week ago so she could be an inspired listener tonight.

I dressed five times, calling a friend, "What do you think? Is the Kamali too weird?" "But it's you," she said.

"That's what I mean." As I changed clothes, I told myself over and over, 'do not tell old Hollywood stories, do not talk about yourself, ask about them.' Do not do astrology. Will Jim call Stuart tomorrow and say, 'you're doing it again.' Stuart hasn't really told me anything about them, except that they once worked together and that he loves them. Do *not* do astrology.

We sat down to a candlelit dinner, several courses of what was coming to be known as nouvelle cuisine. We told about our meeting and falling in love. After dinner, Jill asked Jane and Jim what their astrology signs were, and said, "Of course, you're so romantic, so loving with each other. Where did you begin, and how do you keep it going?"

"Well," Jane said, "Jim feels, and I think there's some truth to it, that we were really fortunate that I had such an awful first marriage."

"Best thing that ever happened to me," Jim said. "If her husband had been an outstanding guy, Jane would have been off-limits for everybody else."

"I was simply not in love," Jane said. "I felt constricted, married for life without love. Horrible."

Then Jim said, "It wasn't love at first sight. At first sight, there was no question that I wanted to get into bed with her, but that's not the same as love. But when I finally did get her into bed, I realized I wanted to be with her the rest of my life. This was the woman for me—if I was for her. I proposed the next day, but it was only later on I discovered that Jane was just as beautiful inside as she is outside."

"It took me a long time to understand the difference between men and women," Jane said. "At first, what made Jim so appealing to me was that I always knew where I stood with him, that he was going to tell the truth. Even if it hurt."

"Did he ever really do that?" Jill asked.

"Why, yes," Jane said, "he told me early on that he couldn't imagine being faithful to one woman for the rest of his life. That shook me up, but it also made me realize that he's not going to be sneaking around, hiding what he's doing."

"But that must have been hard for Jane to take," I said to Jim.

"Yeah," Jim said. "Remember I was young and naïve, twenty-six when I said that. I thought that in a marriage, a guy would occasionally do something with another woman, like on a business trip, meeting a woman in a bar, but it wouldn't mean a damn thing to the marriage."

"I couldn't imagine Jane dealing with that," I said, and looked at Jill, "or Jill."

"That's true," Jane said. "However, Jim, tell Stu and Jill how your thinking evolved."

"Although I thought my attitude was sort of liberated, European, I came to realize that Jane took this matter very seriously. So seriously that I said to her, you don't have to worry about it now that I know how important this is to you."

"So that was good," I said.

"No, not good enough at all," Jim said. "Jane said flatly—I want you to behave not because *I* want you to, but because *you* want to."

I looked at Jane. "I knew you were tough."

"Very tough," Jim agreed, "and because of her toughness, I got pretty well straightened out about fidelity. As I've said before, the secret is to marry someone like Jane."

"Thank you, honey," Jane said. "I'll say something else. It took me a while to understand how central to a man's happiness good sex is. You really have to make him feel you love him all the time.

Jim has often said, 'In all our years together, you've never had a headache.' With that, everything falls into place."

"Let me tell you a story, Jill," Jim went on. "When I was thinking of marriage with Jane, I called Stuart and asked him if he thought it was a good idea. I'd expected him to immediately respond in favor of the idea, but he was silent, contemplating for a while. Then he said, 'Jim, I think this will work. You're highly disciplined and Jane's accommodating and flexible, so it should work.' And Stu was right. That's the way it's been."

"This is perfect," Jill said. "I'm accommodating and flexible, too, and Stuart is disciplined. But that is probably not exactly true with any of us, all the time. My guess is the trouble comes when we insist that something always stays the same. It's rigid expectations that make trouble."

I can see Jill is feeling more at ease. "So, do you have one thing that comes up over and over, one stressful thing?" she asked.

"Children," Jane answered.

"Children," Jim said.

"Perhaps we can talk about this some other time," I suggested.

"I'll drink to that," Jim said.

"Jane and I'll discuss it on the phone," Jill said.

"At length," Jane said.

The moon and stars shone bright and keen in the midnight sky as we left the Holdens for the drive back to my place. We parked on Compo Beach to enjoy a few minutes by the ocean.

"A lovely evening," Jill said, "I think they like me."

"What's not to like—and love," I said, enfolding her in my arms. "My friends are now your friends."

He says these things about children, family, and friends, to hope they will come true. Stuart's more positive, less cynical. Is this, I wonder, a Christian thing? It can only be useful to come in with this attitude. Will Jim and Jane really trust me to be the supportive, consistently loving, and selfless force Jane is in Jim's life, the element Stuart needs? Or do they see how I can be sometimes? I want to say, 'Listen, I really care. I can learn.'

I called my mother that night, after Stuart had gone to sleep. My mother is awake when everyone else isn't, and sleeps when everyone else is awake. My parents were still in love, which was partly what was crushing them, knowing it was almost over. My mother had never taken me too seriously as a feminist, so I knew she'd tell me the truth. Could I be a partner to Stuart, the way Jane is to Jim? A real support system?

"Not easily," she said. "You've always put yourself first. You'll have to put Stuart first, or you'll lose him, too. Is that what you wanted to hear?"

The next day, I drove over to pick Jill up for a ride in the country. "I'm crazy about Jane," she said, "she's direct and real. She's so giving, Stuart. She listens and focuses completely. How clearly they understand you, and love you." She was still bubbling over with the experience of the Holdens' dinner for us last night. "I loved them right away!"

"I can see that," I told Jill. "I think Jane can be a good friend to you, because she's been through this situation, falling in love when you have kids from a former marriage."

We drove and drove, up into New York State, and got to talking about the kids, our kids, sort of reviewing the situation.

"We are not the Brady Bunch," Johanna had pronounced in the first few days of our meeting each other, "and I suppose she's right," I said to Jill.

Jill had Jeremy and Johanna, twenty-one and nineteen. I had Stuart Jr., Susan, and Philip, twenty-nine, twenty-two, and twenty-one. All of us, except Stu Jr., had met already, and I told Jill I saw the relationship geometry something like this.

"Jeremy is suspicious of me because he's fiercely protective of you," I said. "He's not close to his father, but has a strong attachment to his grandfather."

"You and Johanna got along from the start," Jill said. "She is a strong, very generous person who's had to deal with my failures. Her own father's gone, so is Laurie. Johanna's so eager for this to work, for you to be here for her."

"I understand," I said. "My oldest son, Stu Jr., is a classic sixties kid. College dropout, artistic, drugs and LSD. He helped build a hospital in a commune in Nashville, married a girl in the Peace Corps, and had two little boys. They opened up another commune in New Mexico where he now works as a paramedic."

"I think I've caught on to him," Jill said.

"You just identify with him, all the sixties paraphernalia you were both involved with. He's complicated and has an addictive personality," I said. "My daughter, Susan, suffered a lot from my drunken behavior in years gone by, as all my kids did, but remains devoted now that I'm sober."

"She's a careful listener, a real giver," Jill said. "It may be easiest for our daughters to know each other. And Philip I loved right away."

"He's very smart and ambitious," I said. "Part of him probably wants to be the corporate big shot I was. Sometimes I wonder if he may be a little confused by me as a role model with all my drink and sexual shenanigans, but we're close to each other."

"So, is any family really a bunch?" Jill asked. "Or do we love those family stories because they give us an image to aim for."

We were standing on an escarpment high above the Hudson River, looking along the deep, forested gorge, a picture book painting of tranquillity. "I think, Jill, that we love each of our kids in the best way we know how and try to pass on to each of them our experience, strength, and hope, one day at a time."

Nine

❦

Taking Stuart to meet some of my friends, couples I've known for years, felt like a theatrical tryout. Would it play? Would they believe that he loves me? My choices in men were always suspect—what sort of fictional character would I trail by them next?

I sometimes saw myself as a production, an arrangement of gestures and ideas designed for your amusement. How am I playing today? Do you like this story? Give me a minute, I'll pull out the scene I did last night. I was trying to change, to find a world I would fit into.

I belonged to the California land, but I was never really part of L.A. I was fueled by New York's drive. To be a strong writer, you ought to do time in the Village, but even when I lived there, I felt I was only passing through. I loved the Connecticut hills, the winding roads, but then I never really fit into the community of serious Eastern artists and writers.

Now I was on my own, my kids were ready to leave the nest. I needed a partner of some fascination to see me through long winter nights. Perhaps, with an educated Englishman, I could slip into this Connecticut literary world. With Stuart, maybe this will be where I really live.

My friend Sandy wasn't home the first afternoon I dropped by with Stuart, but later she called me, laughing, to report that her husband, Anatole, told everyone at a dinner later that night I'd found a charming, starving English poet who knew Claire Bloom.

"Not starving at all," I told Sandy on the phone, "he guides business companies, something like that."

"It might be something to find out." Sandy got right to the point, as usual.

I figured this new relationship was perfect because I'd told all my favorite stories, I felt I was understood and appreciated. But have I listened? What did I really hear him say about himself? What did I know beyond what I saw, what I've felt?

"He plays piano, jazz, and writes wonderful poetry." I recited a couple of lines I remembered from "The Best Times Were the Talking Times," a love poem he wrote before he met me.

"That's good," Sandy said. Then I told her he'd even stabbed the last woman he loved when she went out on him. "Well, at least he's capable of heavy passion."

We were driving over to Anatole and Sandy Broyard's house in Weston, Connecticut. Jill was unusually quiet, and I got to musing over our different sets of friends and whether we would fit, or not fit, together.

I'd met Lynn and Dick Gilman at dinner last week with their two young daughters, well-mannered sprites. Dick Gilman's the literary critic who teaches at Yale and writes for various magazines. His wife, Lynn Nesbit, a high-powered literary agent, is, in fact, Jill's agent. We had a typical suburban barbecue: salad, hamburgers, and hot dogs.

Dick's erudite and opinionated. I get the feeling that his purist approach may be partly motivated by his need to separate his "serious" work from the popular. I knew he was checking me out. He's protective and paternalistic toward Jill, in the way of a father with a naughty child who just happens to be good at something.

Lynn's a sharp contrast, a tough lady who is all business. She and Dick seem to have a nice relationship, which is probably helped by Lynn's living in New York during the week. Both of them seem to have Jill's best interests at heart. They obviously liked me, but I understand quite clearly that some of this liking must stem from previous unfortunate experiences with Jill's companions.

I have far fewer friends than Jill does. Many of my old drinking companions I've had to forsake or they've given up on me, and many others didn't want to deal with me in my darkest days. The friends I have left are truly through-thick-and-thin friends, like the Holdens and the Gelbs—friendships that have endured for decades.

"I'm looking forward to this Broyard visit," I said. "When we met Anatole a few days ago, I sensed we'd get along just fine."

Anatole was crazy to talk, mostly about a disastrous summer in a rented house in the Dordogne. I know with absolute certainty that he doesn't listen to a word that is said other than his own, but he's a friendly, lively character. He talked incessantly about France and the New York literary scene and his own writing.

"I've never had any trouble moving in different milieus," I told Jill.

"The question is, will you get along with my friends?" Jill said. "They love informal parties, people dropping in, anything to distract from the writing."

"My closest friends have strong marriages," I said, "and are very sociable and give wonderful parties in their lovely homes. You'll see."

I returned to my musing and a few minutes later rather pompously announced, "My first principle in our new set of relationships is this. I will try to befriend anyone who has been supportive of you before we met; I will shun anybody who was not."

"Sounds pretty aggressive." Jill smiled.

"I am pretty aggressive." I smiled back.

Today we were gathered around the glass table on the terrace overlooking the wide lawn, reviewing the hollyhocks and delphiniums in the borders, considering the options of marjoram and thyme, the possibilities of peonies. Dick and Stuart were talking about a new Eliot biography, while the rest of us went on about *Apocalypse Now*, Brando's performance, and the rumors that the production "was more expensive than the actual war."

Sandy, silver-gold strands of hair falling forward, watched as we started eating, wanting Anatole to stop distracting us from the food, but he performed conversations with such flamboyant gestures, flirting with every intimacy. Would you rather eat or watch Anatole talk?

Dick Gilman was everyone's professor. Anatole would have been an irritant if Dick hadn't decided ages ago that Anatole was more an entertainer. Dick was more serious than everyone, which was his seductive approach. You longed to comfort him, make him smile.

Sandy, Lynn, Martha Stewart, and I were talking about the food—wonderful salads, an amazing Stilton brioche. Stuart was listening to Anatole talk about his life in the Village in the late forties. I never knew where to come in on the literary exchange. Stuart didn't have that difficulty. He could throw quotes around fast as anyone.

"Girls wore their souls like negligees they never took off," Anatole said, "and one man in a million knew how to make love to a soul."

I looked over at Stuart. He makes love to my soul. I had not considered my soul for a long time. It's the kind of love that transforms sex. I watched the easy power of his gestures, the engaged expression, his dismissive air. Was this what I had here, and would I have this power inside me? Is the man we love the most the man we would be? Will you be my speed, the animus to drive me on? Stuart has had enough power to throw around. He won't be so fearful that he'll run away when he feels my force.

I considered love in Southport. Did we look at each other's loving? Was that taboo? Anatole and Sandy were opposites. Lynn and Dick shared a moral gravity, a deep respect for principle. Did you fall in love with tastes, with principles? Do we ever know what someone really falls in love with? How did we know we had the fuel to keep going?

Perfect couples. Were they? Were Stuart and I becoming a "perfect couple"? Or was this longing of mine so fierce that I was playing a new role with a sublime costar? Everyone who accepts me understands that I change to fit the scene. Did he see this yet?

I watched his charming manner, the way he is the complete person he is everywhere.

"I didn't make anything fancy today," Sandy said. "If I did, it would be to impress you," she told Martha.

Martha, tall and vigorous, liked her house and dense, plush gardens more than her work on Wall Street. She handed around a potato salad she'd made. "It's just wonderful," she told us, "tiny new potatoes and fresh mint."

Lynn tasted it. "It's good. Isn't this dill bread amazing?" You wanted Lynn to talk about your writing the way she talked about food.

Lynn caught reactions like snapshots with her fast, jet eyes. She grinned with exasperation as Dick continued his discussion with Anatole about a new book, by a man, on women. And love. Anatole raised his eyebrows and flashed his smile to keep Sandy's reserved New England elegance just self-conscious enough.

Dick was explaining the philosophy behind a play he'd just critiqued. "Dick," Lynn was brisk, "we're eating now."

As Martha and Lynn battled their way through a conversation about real estate values in Weston and Fairfield, like high school champions going for the trophy, Anatole suggested Dick could turn it into a play. "About land wars. It's your turn to write a play," he said, but Dick encouraged everyone except himself.

And, then, nothing Dick heard, nothing you said, was exactly right, which was why he was an excellent critic. He'd find the flaw and gently point it out. Lynn's sharp insights made me flinch. When she and I first met, she told me, "Stop writing these little magazine pieces and write that story you have to tell." She changed my life.

Anatole enjoyed taking stances in opposition to Dick, mostly to tease him and to enjoy the wordplay. Like star students, they jousted, positioning ideas for battle. Dick said, "The novel is only a medium for a new kind of truth and pleasure—it's not about bringing on social change—that's an outdated notion."

"It seems to me," I said, "that writers, novelists have always been at the forefront of social change—from Richardson to Dickens, to Orwell and Huxley. It would be difficult for me to comprehend a world in which novelists were not relating to the massive social changes that will be brought about by revolutionaries and counterrevolutionaries, by scientific and technological advances."

Suddenly, without warning, Anatole turned to me and asked, "So who is your favorite poet? Auden? Everybody in the Village likes Auden."

"I'm not in the Village," I said quickly, "and I don't like Auden much at all, either poetically or politically. Among my favorites are Eliot and Baudelaire and Pope."

"What's your favorite line from Pope?" Anatole pressed me.

"Words are like leaves and where they most abound much fruit of sense beneath is rarely found."

"And Baudelaire?" he kept pressing.

"*Hypocrite lecteur, mon semblable, mon frère.*"

"Touché, Stuart!" exclaimed Dick, "your game."

On the way home, Stuart's attention was fixed on the dark, winding road. I was charged up by his authority. Do tough women fall in love or cinch a good deal when they see it coming? Do smart people lay the cards on the table and see the facts and say, "Well, this should work," and call it "love"?

"Maybe true love," I said, "is the attachment so deep that nothing will break it apart—not anger, not embarrassment, not the boredom of ordinary days, no dumb, quick making it with someone else on a business trip. But a man wouldn't tell if he did it when he was really in love, would he?" I looked over at him, a little anxiety here.

"Oh? How about you don't do it with someone else when you're really in love," Stuart said.

I wouldn't, but men do. Do men fall in love like we do? Maybe men just see no point in talking over what they can't fix. Like channel surfing; if you don't like it, you switch. We keep on watching and watching and watching, figuring something may get better. We keep talking about the longing, the issue, the trouble, over and over, figuring we can see it in a new way.

That night, Martha called to tell me I could come pick up some raspberries from her garden. "I'm starting a catering business, so if you guys are thinking of getting married, keep me in mind. I'd love to do your wedding."

So, they *can* see. He really loves me.

Ten

Falling in love is one thing, and Viking blood oaths are certainly another, but marriage is quite a different thing, especially when there's a failed marriage in your past. I'd had one of those and Jill had been through two, yet both of us very quickly came to the idea of marriage.

It happened like this.

Jill and I were, as usual, at the seven-thirty A.M. meeting, but unusually, we were smartly dressed in summer white for an appointment in Manhattan. As we left the meeting, a friend commented, "You and Jill look as though you could be going off to be married." "You mean, after only a month?" and we laughed and drove away.

We were chatting aimlessly with radio jazz in the background. On the surface, we were talking about living arrangements, when suddenly our previous talk about not needing marriage sounded hollow. I realized that I'd been fooling myself. My friend's comment about marriage stuck in my head, and I felt amazingly energized by the pounding dynamics of the music, "Birdland" by the Weather Report.

"Goddammit, then!" I exploded. "Will you marry me?"

Jill threw herself around me, "Yes, yes, yes, you idiot. Of course I will."

The radio blasts sounded like high-tech coronation music. We'd have danced in the car if it were possible!

"We've got to get you a ring," I shouted over the music.

"Yes, please," she said, "and we'll figure out a date later. Our sponsors will, no doubt, tell us we shouldn't make major decisions so early, but we'll deal with that later."

We found a treasury of antique rings at a tiny jewelry store near Bloomingdale's. Boxes and boxes of antique rings. I saw the right one instantly, but looked at others to give Stuart a chance to make his choice. "Don't play with me," he said, "this is the one."

It was an old Cartier ring with what is really a Virgo sign on it, but we both read the symbol as the Roman numeral XII to echo the twelve-step program. Then we had a romantic little lunch at Le Veau d'Or, a French restaurant he said reminded him of places he knows in Paris, "places I will take you one day." Cold salmon for me, blanquettes de veau a l'ancienne for him. He loves French cooking, which is like food in lingerie. I'll learn to like it.

I proposed to Jill in French, put the ring on her finger, and wrote my proposal on a little map of Paris card we found on the table. We were dramatizing the engagement in a good old-fashioned way.

"So, we should see your parents right away," I said to Jill. "Manners, tradition, and all that."

"Great idea," she agreed.

My parents will be pleased to see this is real, and my mother will be *so* surprised. She may not remember her advice to me about putting Stuart first. She was tough, but the hardest hitting advice goes deep and stays there. The truth about loving is if you put each other first, you come up with a kind of balance. I think I believe this, but you have to be sure he is putting you first, too.

Stuart and I walked slowly through the hideous New York heat to their apartment building with its vast tiled lobby. My father's secretary answered the door.

My mother always had a small dog to which I was allergic, and my father always had a secretary who wore high heels. His secretary's major role now was to reflect, as an audience does, the power of my parents' romantic attachment to each other. Lois, their housekeeper, had done that for years. She was the in-house audience, wearing old house slippers, except when Mayor Lindsay came to call.

My father's hair was soft, not combed back. He had on blue slacks, a crumpled white linen shirt open at the neck. This was his writing look. Even though he had a meeting in an hour, he was easy and pleased to see Stuart again, another man in the world who did not wear jeans. He took one look at my grin and the way I was clasping Stuart's arm. "To what do I owe the pleasure of this lovely visit?" he asked, and called my mother to join us.

Miriam made an entrance, glamorously attired in a silky long jacket and pants outfit. I was startled to see her without her wig, her sparse brown hair flat against her head, which made her look like a medieval Madonna or an early American primitive.

"I'm too old, Mr. Schary, to ask your permission," I said, "but I certainly want to advise you before anyone else that I love your daughter, I have asked her to marry me, and today we have become engaged."

Dore congratulated us both, shook my hand, embraced me once, and again, even closer, and kissed Jill so warmly, so happily.

Jill showed her mother her ring. Miriam kissed Jill, embraced me, and said, "I never thought I'd have another son-in-law, not for Jill." She turned to Jill, "You'll be protected, as well as loved."

"Which is exactly my oath to Jill," Stuart said, "to love and protect her." My father said, "Wait," and left the room for a moment. Then Stuart stood up as my father came back wearing his wonderful bolo tie. Its slide had a gray-blue stone the color of my father's eyes. As Daddy stood before Stuart and lifted the bolo from around his neck, Stuart latched on instinctively to the dynamics of the scene. He snapped to rigid attention, gave a swift military salute to my father, and said, "Merci, mon Général." Daddy's sense of theater emerged, and he returned the salute.

Suddenly, standing before this new man of mine, my father was fragile. He was tall, but with a new bend forward in his stance; a birch tree after a storm. And there was the translucence of his skin.

"So," Daddy said to Stuart now, "I suppose I should be asking you all kinds of questions," but he didn't. Maybe because he wasn't strong enough anymore to worry, or he was embarrassed to talk about money, to which the questions were likely to lead. Either my family had money and spent it quickly, making grand gestures—or it had none at all, and there was profound embarrassment at being unable to care for everyone.

"Did you see the Yankees last night?" my father asked. "That great play in the seventh. . . ." He glanced at me and laughed. "Or did Jill have you otherwise engaged."

My father was relieved, I'd met my match. I wanted to throw my arms around him and say, 'This doesn't mean you can go now.'

I showed Stuart the room where my mother painted, the photographs of her Russian grandparents and family. There was one I loved, around a formal luncheon table set in a garden, the women in gowns and hats and feathers, the men all fierce, mustached, and tragic-looking. *"The Cherry Orchard,"* Stuart said.

There was very little from the Hollywood years, which I hadn't allowed myself to see until Stuart pointed it out later. You get a different perspective showing someone else around. There were the signed photographs from Presidents Roosevelt, Truman, and Kennedy, and posters from my father's plays.

We came back into the living room to find that the backers had arrived to see my father about his new musical, and the set designer was waiting to go over sketches. As Stuart and I were leaving, my father held me close and told Stuart he'd like to take us to the theater. Then, as he turned to go back to his gathering, he seemed stronger, glowing with a producer's bravado.

Eleven

I had wanted Jill to meet my oldest American friends, Bruce and
Lueza Gelb, not only because of the friendship, but because they
represented a family with values that I cherished. I suppose I was
really saying that I still knew some decent people after my dark
years and dubious companions.

The Gelbs had four bright and attractive children, two boys
and two girls, and were very family oriented and community
minded. I can remember Bruce, back in Cincinnati when we
were together at P&G, dragging me to make door-to-door calls
for the United Appeal, while I was moaning about the virtues of
socialized medicine—not a popular position during the 1950s
Cold War. Bruce left P&G because he wanted to work at Clairol,
the company started by his own family. I remembered how supportive a wife Lueza was, and how super competent she was—at
tennis, badminton, swimming, waterskiing—and sailing.

I was pleased when the Gelbs invited us for a day on Long
Island Sound on their boat, which they moored close to my place

in Southport, at the Pequot Yacht Club. A perfect sunny day with a light breeze.

Lueza could, I'm sure, skipper this yacht single-handed around the Horn. There she stands, golden hair flying in the breeze, behind the wheel, laughing at just the joy of it, the spray, and the rail skimming low, almost in the waves. Bruce, tall, dark, and handsome, is, as usual, filled with nervous energy and is everywhere, greeting us, waving to buddies, hauling on lines, loading canvas bags of food.

Bruce and Lueza, here in action on their boat, are the perfect way for Jill to be introduced to my friends.

Sailing is elegant action. As the boat slipped out across the sound, with Lueza Gelb taking the wheels, Bruce the sails, I felt I was on a steady, new course. Bruce and Lueza have managed to stay married and keep their family ties strong and their lives private.

I was in love with a sailing man once. I look at Stuart here in the sun, talking to Bruce, and I go back to long, quiet hours on the Pacific with the gentle reverie you can only get about former lovers when you're in sight of a safe, new shore. Part of the trouble then was the collision course between my late adolescence and that man's children's need for his attention. Like all relationships, with every twist of the kaleidoscope you see another picture, and they're all true. I wanted my kids to be the only kids in my life, so when we broke up, it had little to do with whether we were crazy about each other.

I am thinking about this carefully, because tomorrow Stuart is going to Cincinnati for his daughter's graduation. He will be sitting with Margaret, watching their daughter. I can imagine how moved they will be. They'll touch each other's hands. I can make him really crazy and uncomfortable about this if I try, put enough electricity into him before the trip so he'll be uneasy, and then relieved to be with his own serene family. Stop, I tell myself.

Lueza and I made sandwiches. She's a guy's perfect woman, lean and tan, and not into fussing. She looks as though she just pulled a shirt and shorts out of the drawer this morning without giving it too much thought. 'No fuss' is the fundamental elegance.

After we finished lunch, Lueza returned to the sailing. She told me she was writing a book about her childhood on Schroon Lake, and I thought how our parents' love stories folded into our own expectations, like ingredients sifted into the batter.

"I don't think most couples ever hear 'for better or worse.' You have to keep your mind and your heart on the fact you have a family. You're not two lovebirds."

This is the opposite of what my mother told me before my first marriage. 'Just be his lover. Don't be his wife. Don't talk about money, the kids, or the house. Just adore him.'

Lueza and I agreed you really can't come up with a guide that's going to work for every marriage. The only way you learn is by hearing stories about how other people get through marriage, knowing when to talk and when to shut up with him and get on the phone with your mom or a girlfriend.

"You can tell a lot from photographs," I said. "Do you have old family pictures?"

"I have my parents' courting photo from 1918," Lueza said. "Mother is twenty-one, her bobbed hair dips slightly over one eye. She looks happy, but shy. Daddy is twenty-six, mouth straight and closed, his eyes crinkling slightly, perhaps the beginning of a smile. He is dressed in a three-piece banker's suit, watch chain and all. He stands straight, in charge, facing Mother. Do you have pictures of your parents before they were married?"

"Lots," I said. "I have one picture of my mother looking so radiant, just after my father proposed. She was wearing a beaded chiffon gown, 'Alice blue,' she always said, 'but I can't remember who the Alice was.'"

"Oh, I know," Lueza said. *"My sweet little Alice blue gown*—it was a song about the color of Alice Roosevelt Longworth's eyes."

"Yes," I said, "and the quality of this photograph made my mother's eyes gleam, and her hair seemed made of moonlight. My mother always wanted to go to Europe on her honeymoon. She wound up with my father in the Catskills at a camp for underprivileged boys, where he was a counselor. I have a picture of my parents in their bathing suits. He looks like a roughneck, and starving. They're both raw, eager for each other."

"There's a picture of my parents in 1920," Lueza said, "a young couple in funny flapper bathing suits. My mother's looking straight into the camera. Daddy's expression is almost the same as before. Such a good-looking man, and Mother was beautiful, but I wonder, what were they really like?"

"Maybe that's what we want from our parents," I said, "some mystery. Do we want to be so intimate, after all?"

"Maybe not." Lueza considered that.

I tasted the salt spray from my fingertips. "I don't imagine Stuart and Bruce are talking about their parents like this," I said.

"No," Lueza agreed, "women are different that way."

Lueza is an ideal influence for me. I doubt if she would fuss if Bruce was going on a trip somewhere, and it would probably never cross her mind that he might not come back. I guess I will have some fear when I'm apart from Stuart because of all the times Laurie didn't come back. The thing is to get more used to the idea that Stuart *will* come home, than I am to the idea that he might not.

"You and Lueza make a hell of a good crew," I said to Bruce.

"And this time, Stu, you seem to have found a great shipmate in Jill. Somebody with that literary side that has always intrigued you. You're a romantic, and that's probably what gives you the keen perception of women's motivations that make you a terrific marketing man."

"I could say that about you, too, Bruce, in spades. You have a strong mother, a real wife and mother of your children, and your entire business life is about appealing to women—'Does she or doesn't she?' and all that jazz."

"So, we're both romantics," Bruce said. "In fact, for us, talking about business is talking about women, and perhaps women don't get that when they dismiss us with lines like 'oh, they're just talking business.'"

"Yes," I said, "it's like conversing in code or Sanskrit, while women are painting these wonderful Impressionist canvases with all their nuances and intimate touches."

"Vive la différence," Bruce said. "And that's one of the keys to a strong relationship—recognising that there are legitimate and critical differences between men and women, and that there's not a right way and a wrong way, just different ways."

"Agree," I said. "I'll try to remember that."

Once again it strikes me how close Bruce and I were in our feelings and how rarely we talk about them. Not because we're unable to talk, Lord knows, but because we seem to be so often on the same wavelength. We assume a lot and we trust our "instincts," which are often the sum total of our experiences in similar situations. And, with women, a genuinely talented marketing person is continually refreshing his understanding of the audience by constant contact, questioning, probing the attitudes, reaching for the psyche. Bruce is really good at all this.

That night, after we drove home from the yacht club in Southport, Jill and I walked along Compo Beach. I knew she was trying not to talk about my leaving tomorrow to see Susan. She was trying to be very calm, and I could feel the effort.

"Today, sailing with the Gelbs, was wonderful," Jill said. "What I really want," and I heard the catch of tears, "is to go on sailing forever into the horizon, just the two of us, free and in love on the ocean, alone."

"I suddenly have this mental image from years ago in Jamaica, on the beach at Negril," I said, putting my arm around her shoulder as we walked. "There was a man walking up and down the beach, proudly, his left forearm bending toward the sea, as though his shells on the wooden platter were pulling to go back. The tilt of his body suggested an African warrior bearing gifts to a prince or some noble feudal lord. Maybe this is the beginning of some sort of mystical connection. I see you passing through my life like a shadow going through a shadow. I see two people as superimposed kaleidoscopes, randomly matching up on a red diamond here, blue square there, yellow circle over here, and only the most fleeting of instants where the patterns mesh precisely."

"What I don't want," Jill said, "is to be just passing through."

• • •

Of my three children, Susan was undoubtedly affected the most by my troubled times; leaving Cincinnati, the big house, Chicago Latin School, the divorce, living with her mother. But she remained fiercely loyal to me, even coming to live with me in Connecticut for her last year in high school.

Susan was instrumental in getting me into my final rehab. She was tired of my evasions and denials, and finally exploded when I was supposed to be straight and she saw me glugging a bottle of vodka. Minutes later she was driving me to Norwalk Hospital, the psych ward. Susan saved my life, I'm sure of that.

So I was flying to Cincinnati where Susan was graduating with her B.A. Susan and Philip were at the airport to meet me, and they drove me to her apartment, clearly the den of a writer. I could comfortably have moved right in—the books, the desk, the typewriter, stereo, magazines. Susan had worked out a way of living independently with Winston, her German shepherd. What's more, she already had a job as a cultural coordinator in southern Ohio.

Glancing at the Virginia Woolf calendar over the desk, I said, "Yes, Susan, a room of one's own and fifty pounds a year." I could sense Susan's emergence as a capable and determined woman. "Tomorrow your graduation gift, and your freedom may be complete." The gift, a Ford Escort loaded with options, promptly christened Scoop.

The kids wanted to eat at the Maisonette, Cincinnati's best restaurant. Nostalgia trip. "All our anniversaries had been celebrated here," I reminded them.

"Oh, Dad," said Susan, "this is actually where I started to be born, wasn't it?"

Margaret, nine months pregnant, and I had been dining here

with a friend when her water broke and we had to rush her to the hospital for the delivery. "But what you probably didn't know, Susie," I said, "is that we planned to call you Maisie, after the Maisonette, but we thought better of it." It was nostalgia and laughter all the way.

I slept in Susan's bed, and she took a sleeping bag on the floor. Before sleep, she sat at her desk, typing a paper she was working on, throwing words at me for spelling. Later in the night, I looked at her asleep in the sleeping bag, the trusty dog beside her. It had been such a journey, such a period of adjustment for my little girl.

My last image of her as I left for the airport was a young woman wearing jeans and a French beret, posed on the hood of her car. I love her dearly. She is a gritty survivor, and I am filled with gratitude that my sobriety has opened the way back to me for my children. Of one thing I'm sure. You should never, ever give up trying to devise a loving relationship with your children, and the love you give must feed their independence, not any needs of your own.

Twelve

I met Stuart and Philip at The Stock Exchange, a genuine smashed piano-bar scene. Helen was there, of course, and all over Stuart. One of Stuart's friends caught this, winks at me. We came home late and Stuart said, in the jazz guy drawl I hate, "Helen called me today."

"Listen, I put up with your being so neat and right about everything so I can be around your style and hear your English accent," I said. "I don't want a Norwalk trucker."

"Helen thought she'd stop by because John's away." His accent's back, completely James Mason here. "I picked up some sexual overtones from her while we were driving down to the club, and I thought about how that might be with her and it bothered me. Even thinking about it bothered me." He was rather pleased with himself. "I've changed a lot."

Silence. Telling me this may have been a mistake.

"I knew it!" I blew up. "She hates me! She had her eyes on you the whole time."

"You're clearly not secure enough for this kind of talk." He became the fierce governess, so very English now.

"Don't throw it back on me, make it my problem. She's needy and cunning, getting guys to feel sorry for her while she undercuts other women."

"You're just being vicious. She's a misunderstood kid."

"Exactly what she wants you to think!" I stood straight, hands on hips, body at its best angle—see what you're going to lose.

He saw, but he was furious. "What's honesty worth between people who love each other if we can't discuss our innermost thoughts? Either one of us can have a sexy thought about anyone else. It's called a fantasy. Only repressed fantasies get sublimated in actions. I'd a hell of a lot rather have you *talk* out a fantasy than *act* it out!"

"But I don't want to hear it, and you're threatening me. Either I hear it or you'll act it out. Wonderful!" I looked around for something to throw, to punctuate.

"I can't understand that kind of pussyfooting around. You're always making little veiled references to your former boyfriends, and I deal with it. I am not going to be upset because somebody else fucked you, so it's crazy for you to go wild because I imagine someone else."

We were silent—a stormy silence. He stretched out flat on the brown leather couch in the living room. I left the room, went into the bedroom. Don't do this. I went back into the living room, "What are you thinking?"

"Crazy thoughts and ideas. You've pushed my buttons, misinterpreted my honesty—what else?—restricted my freedom. Our relationship is in jeopardy."

I was crying, sitting on the side of the couch with my back to him.

I took a bottle of vodka some visitors had left behind and set it down on the kitchen table. With the bottle staring us both in the face, I told Jill that the thing we had to keep uppermost in our minds at all times was that keeping the cork in this bottle is the most important thing in our lives. After that, next most important, were our feelings for each other—the rest is propaganda. It cleared the air.

"We're really too tired," he said, "the whole day has been over-programmed. Shall we talk about our wedding?" He kissed me.

"Oh, tomorrow," I said. Easy does it. "Let's get some sleep, or something."

"Yes, definitely something," he said, and led me into the bedroom.

The next morning, early enough so I knew it was at the end of a long night for him, my second husband called. Laurie? How many years had it been? He wanted some letters he never left behind.

"I never had them, or you never left them. You took anything that was yours," I was glad Stuart was here so I could be clear and direct. He was watching me carefully. "Laurie, you can't just call me like it was yesterday, after disappearing years ago." Of course he could, that was Laurie. "I've fallen in love with someone else," I told him, "you and I are completely over."

"I was shattered by him, but I never hated him," I said to Stuart after I hung up. I loved Stuart for sitting here, not getting angry, catching on to all my conflicts without being threatened. Could I be like that? "I guess the memories of someone you once loved stay," I said, "and you trip over them now and then, like accidents. Can't be helped."

"You understand this with you," Stuart said, "but you don't understand this when it happens to me, like when I see someone from the past and *I* say, 'There's nothing there.'"

"But there's always something," I said, "you know that—and with you there's more. I know how powerfully you commit to people, how completely you care."

"Listen," he said, "only a few days ago we were lying right here when my old girlfriend called. Now Zoe and Laurie have both been dealt with honestly and openly."

That simple. How smart is that?

Then the phone rang again. "Hello," I growled. Then, to Stuart, "it's Helen." Before I could hand the phone over, she said, "How good it was to see you folks last night, you're really neat." "Thanks," I said, handing the phone to Stuart. I am not *really neat.*

When he hung up, he thought I was being remorseful for suspecting her, when I was only on guard in a wiser way: make love now. Afterward, he brushed at my forehead with his fingertips and said, "It's clear to me that I do have something of a problem with your attitudes toward my old relationships."

"I should hope so," I said. "I could pretend not to give a damn."

Playing with Jill in the moonlight. Fingers caress, enter, explore, sensing the changing shapes and textures within. Old fantasies of Georgia O'Keeffe orchids now transmute into fashion, intimate outfits as works of art. And this is the changing room for a show of sensory runway costumes. At first tight and enclosed—is this tunic too confining?—then later, delighted with stroking fingers, opened for deeper plunges into Miyake pleats. A maze of warm folds in cottons so fine and silks so smooth, with touches of chambray, pongee, and shantung. Yet silky above all. Yes. A flowing, pink silk gown from, let's imagine, Balenciaga. Yes, yes.

Now in her drop-dead fullness she takes charge of the show. She knows exactly where to strut, twist, and turn, command the scene, reaching for what she now knows is reachable. Right there at runway's end she trembles, quivers with the delight of success, gasps with the relief of achievement. Within her there is a tumult of appreciation, fluttering gently into whisper before, after the briefest pause, she reappears in yet another stunning outfit.

We were lying in my four-poster log bed and I was looking at the moon and stars through the skylight, feeling his heat around me, his body rugged, like my house. This house was perfect. That was a subject we weren't going near—yet. I was not moving. I was not leaving this house.

I did not like Jill's house and I was not moving into it.

Thirteen

"Do we have to take I-95?" I asked. "I like the Merritt." The parkway had more trees, took longer. We were in Stuart's Wagoneer, driving back from the city.

"The Merritt takes longer," Stuart said. Firm.

"I know. I want to have more time together. You're going away on business." I didn't have to ask. Stuart was cranky like this when he had to pull away to become the businessman. "So, you got the Coca-Cola deal?"

"No, that hasn't come through yet," he said, "this client is in Pennsylvania." He looked over at me. "I have an early morning flight. You have to get used to that."

"But I am," I said, "it's just hard when you don't talk about your work. Why didn't you tell me?"

"I'm telling you now. I didn't think you were that interested," he said. "We spend more time talking about writing, which is largely what I do in my work anyway."

I knew he was worried about a new consulting deal with Coca-

Cola, worried that if he got the job, we'd be apart more and I'd be on edge, certain he wouldn't come back each time he'd leave. If he didn't get the job, we'd both be scared about money. He worried more. I'd had more years being broke, I knew you got through it.

We were trying carefully to build a bridge between our worlds, build a new world altogether. The first night we met when he told me about his years at Procter & Gamble, he showed me a picture of his house, a mansion with acres of beautiful gardens. "I adored that house," he said, "but I lost it with everything else I squandered at that time of my life."

He wanted to make a lot of money again. That was what he said, but I knew, deeply, that he really wanted to write. But did *I* want him to write? Or did I want him to make money and give us some security, even if it meant he would be away a lot?

"Do you think I won't understand what you do?" I said to Stuart.

"No," he said, "it's pretty simple. I'm a troubleshooter. I go into a business, find out what's wrong, and try to fix it. The answers to the problems are always somewhere in the organization. I just have to find them and then try to get them implemented."

"That must be really appealing to people already in the company—to have some stranger come in, sizing them up."

"I seem to have a talent for getting along with folk," he said.

As easy as that, he says "folk." He fits right in, which is his gift. Look how he handles the road. Clear, fast, he finds a lane and owns it. That's why he likes freeways. On the parkway you have to find more angles, work the road. That's *my* game. Everything with him is just as direct. Declarative sentence answers. How will this actually work? Will I complicate him? Or will he simplify me? Choose one.

"Most people can recognize a good answer to a problem when they see one," he continued. "If they don't, they let me go."

I'd heard him in conversations with clients—his accent shifted, he could be from Chicago. In an artful way, he became the insider with the perspective only a real outsider could maintain. Maybe you had to understand that about yourself before you could make a brave move to another country. I'd be an outsider in his world, an observer, the way I was an outsider in the East, a Westerner away from my territory.

He pulled up in his driveway, parked his green Wagoneer by my red Cherokee. The cars were good together. I didn't want to go home tonight. I'd just lie there thinking about his going away. Had I learned to stay in the moment? I remembered the times Laurie would go away for a couple of days and come home a couple of months later.

We were having another cigarette under the street lamp to have a little more time together. "It's late for you to drive home. Why don't you stay tonight." He really knew me.

"I wanted you to say that." I put my head on his shoulder, my arm around his body. Is this dancing or clutching? "I could go with you next week, see Philadelphia, The Liberty Bell. But you probably do these trips better on your own—you really want to be alone?" Was there an edge to my voice?

Later in bed I told her, "What you're really scared about, Jill, is this. When I want to be by myself, to disengage, does it mean I want to disengage from you? Not at all, but you've got to understand the difference, my need to be separate, on my own."

"Then maybe we'll make a plan," she said. "You'll have time on your own even when it's not work, time to write. We'll have alternate nights together. Theatrical couples do that when one's in a play in the city. We can keep our own houses, that makes sense."

"Later." I turned toward her. "We'll think about that later. Come here."

Fourteen

Stuart wrote at a simple driftwood desk. Whether it was poetry or a proposal for a corporation, he wrote on yellow lined pads in ink. His assistant, Sally, worked in another room. She wasn't in love with him, exactly, but she sized me up like a mother-in-law. I didn't quite do. I tried bringing flowers. "I don't much care for ornamentation in the office, thank you so much ever the same."

When she finished typing something, Sally placed it on the round table near Stuart's desk. I'd moved the papers slightly to make room for the flowers. "Stuart doesn't like his work moved." She adjusted the pages in perfect order. "The last woman read some and that was it." She shifted her hips and tossed her blond hair with the back of her hand. "That was that. He's a very orderly man."

"Thanks for the tip," I said, "I'll keep that in mind." My instinct was to fling the papers around the room. I just straightened one little batch of papers more to the right with a smart, firm little whisk. "There," I said, "that's better now. Honey," I called out moments later, "I've got your coffee," just so she got the drift that I was on the way into the bedroom. So I won today.

"She's crazy about you"—I sat on the foot of his bed—"and you can't see it. It's unbearable for both of us."

"That's not how it is. Don't patronize me." Stuart sized up my game right away. "Sally likes me working here, quietly with her. We had a working pattern she's used to. Change is difficult, it takes time."

"And so I'm in the way?"

"Right now you are." He looked at me over his glasses.

If a man's assistant has worked with him while he's a bachelor, he's not going to enjoy much peace between her and a new woman. One has to go. Sally went, but not without tears on both sides.

I was looking over a paper he'd just finished, "Corporate Culture." "I like the idea of this," I said.

"You haven't read it." He put it down.

"And I guess I'm not going to."

"Not now." He sat at his breakfast table, hands folded in front like an insurance executive in one of those trust-me-I'm-distinguished ads.

I thought this was strictly a woman's problem, the man's assistant who sees her as the rival invader. Stuart had just as much trouble with the people who worked with me. The character of the problem was different, but everything would have to change. At my house, I saw a cheerful, communal spirit, and he saw chaos. (He saw his assistant as a dedicated hard worker, and I saw a fanatic recluse.)

This is an aspect of corporate culture—what kind of ambiance we want. I won't talk about music, since the music in my house with Stuart will be jazz, not old movie scores. Already, the jazz sounds like him. Do I love music because of its associations for me, and will I grow to prefer jazz because of him? Is this a variation on the theme of compromise? Hang with it long enough, and it will suit you, too.

"Ambiance," I said. I look through the kitchen door framing his pictures and the depressing brown leather couch. Do you choose this color? Or do you walk into a store, say you need a couch, and they can get you this one by Wednesday at a third off?

"You're thinking of my furniture," he said.

"Not thinking of it one way or another," I lied, "just looking it over."

"Sizing it up? What is a house that is ours, yours and mine, going to look like?"

"Maybe it's two houses. That's a reason mine is ideal. You can do some of it the way you want . . ."

"Listen," he said, and I think I've heard him say this before, "it's not the things you have, not just the disorder, the size of the house, or its location. You spend half your time arranging for repairs that don't work. That cuts into your work time. I won't have it cutting into mine."

Fifteen

~

"I don't know where we went wrong
But the feeling's gone
And I just can't get it back"

I came over early. He was singing in the shower. There were pages on his writing table, a story he sent in for the Nelson Algren Award.

The Rio Bar at eight o'clock in the morning never looks as though its stage has been seriously disturbed from one day to the next. The scene changes only in details. Today, I notice, sagged on this corner stool, a hundred years old hag of indeterminate color shriveled to the size of her shopping bag. Another day an aging black junkie had nodded away until he slid off the stool to the floor, like a Slinky toy. The large composition of the set never varies.

There is a long bar on the right as you enter, stools almost all occupied, a few folks standing. Unlike the brawling night time crowd, always up and down, the early morning people are sitters, needing the support, arses soundly on stool, elbows running into the bar, steadying as much of everything that can be steadied against the shakes. The movement is in the bartenders, both swift and inhuman, not friendly, neighborhood bartenders.

"Vodka and chaser." There are no pleasantries, just the order and the cash. This is not a social hour: this is the brutally efficient recharging of rundown, self-destruction battery cells; this is clamping jumper cables from energy bottles to central nervous systems; this is intravenous tubes pumping grain alcohol into malnutritioned veins.

"I didn't hear you come in," I had my towel wrapped around me. She was sitting at my desk, reading. She was startled. I turned down the Gordon Lightfoot tape.

"I didn't know you could sing," she said, "but it's clear you can write." She put down the pages. "This knocks me over."

"That's done," I said, and took the pages and put them back on the desk.

"Yes." She was behind me, hands reaching around. "Don't get dressed," she whispered.

We were lying together, her clothes tossed over the chair, across the floor. I'd turned the tape back on. She took my cigarette to light her own.

"What are you working on now," she asked, "or don't you talk about it?"

"It's my novel. I haven't found the opening yet. I thought music might help. I was latching on to the lyrics, 'but the feeling's gone and I just can't get it back.'"

Jill turned on her side and put her arms around me, "I think I'd like it best if you'd write your own real, tough life, or maybe that's because that's what I understand best."

"Could the fear you sense in my writing be about a fear of getting so deeply involved with you?" I asked. "Could that frighten me on some level?" This may not have been the best thing to say.

"Why?" She touched my jaw lightly. "I didn't think I'd scare you."

"Don't you worry about losing your freedom?"

"No, I worry about losing my writing. I wonder, 'Will it be there the next time? Tomorrow? Next week?' I am always different, and never enough."

"We're both scared, then," I said.

"That's writing," she said.

"Perhaps, Jill, we can share our fears about writing, help each other with them."

"Perhaps," she said.

"Remember, it's my dad's birthday dinner today in New York, and you said you'd take Johanna and me in to do some shopping before we meet up with my parents."

"Fine, I have to make a business call and get a haircut. And thanks for the help with my writing. That's a good feeling."

There was one exception to Jill's perception about human relationships: her relationship with her daughter, Johanna. Jill and I had talked about Johanna, her health and attitudes. Johanna had already had a recurrence of her Crohn's disease since we'd met, and Jill and I had made the first of what would be many trips to see Johanna in the hospital. Johanna's trouble never led to trouble between Jill and me. In fact, caring for somebody else had a bonding effect and, vicariously, it provided me with the feeling of parenting a child of Jill's.

On the drive down to Manhattan, there were undercurrents: Johanna's frustration with the job she took after her disease made it difficult to continue college classes, and Jill's frustration with

Johanna's inability to decide what she wanted to do with her life. War broke out between the two of them.

"You could encourage me to go back to college, if college ever interested you," Johanna said.

"Do I need to feel guilty about that, too?" Jill snapped. "Don't throw everything at me because you can't decide what you want to do."

Johanna fiendishly offered the point of view that she could decide to be a speed freak and a drunk, teach her children how to shoplift, screw up a couple of marriages and a variety of relationships, and perhaps be lucky enough to write a couple of successful novels. Zowie!

"Jill," I finally said, "when we learn we can't control other people, that includes our own kin."

"She can't fix my disease," Johanna talked around her mother, which she knew Jill hated, "so, of course, it's her fault. She can't understand this is *my problem. I* have it. *I* live with it. *I* deal with it."

We dropped Johanna off. Our planned visit to Jill's shrink, Gloria, turned out to be well timed. Gloria, swathed in swirls of fabric which gave her a Colette look, brooding and wise, wasted no time in getting at the deeper issue underlying all Jill's tensions.

"Jill, do you think it is possible for you to have a man who loves you *and* a successful career?"

"I don't really know," Jill mumbled as though not wanting me to hear her, "but I think I might lose the man."

"What do you think, Stuart?" Gloria asked.

"Well, I'm pretty new to this scene, but I do know that Jill is a very vulnerable and insecure person. And yet, of all her fears, I suspect the least important one is about her writing ability. I think this is the talent she feels most confident about."

"Good, Stuart," said Gloria. "Now, Jill, consider this. If you should ultimately choose writing success over a man who loves you, it may well be—on your track record—the writing talent stays with you and the man does not."

"So, where do we go from here?" asked Jill.

"Simple to say," said Gloria, "but not easy to achieve. You must convince yourself that you can write successfully and have a loving relationship at the same time. In fact, I feel that you could get to the point at which the reassurance of your loving relationship will actually enhance your confidence in the writing.

"And Stuart," she added, "never forget. When something is troubling Jill, it is almost always THE BOOK. Always THE BOOK. Always THE BOOK."

"I think I've got it, Gloria," I said. "Always THE BOOK."

In one way or another, life is all about the drama of families. In the case of Jill's family, life was all about the melodrama of family. I assumed that this would be a permanent condition. Perhaps "pathology" is a better word than "condition."

Dore and Miriam arrived in a cab at the restaurant, followed by Jeremy and his girlfriend. Dore, as usual, was very proper, and Miriam was chic in a blond wig and lovely silk dress. She was shaking badly, as if in a palsy state. Jeremy, very much in the mode of his grandfather, was in account executive rig. His girlfriend's pretty, fine-boned face was a strange counterpoint to Miriam's facial paralysis. Johanna was wearing some new drop-dead heels and Jill was understated glamorous.

I was making mental notes on appearances, because the scene struck me as being one in which each person was a commentary on someone else, a nod to power or glamour, a tip of the hat to respect or a nose thumbed at it. All that messy mélange called family; dynamics of possession or rejection.

Jill had arranged for red, white, and blue flowers on the birthday table, Dore's favorite colors, the symbol of the patriotic immigrant. So the table initially seemed festive enough, Dore regaling us all with Hollywood anecdotes from his upcoming book, *Heyday.* We pretended not to notice Miriam's shakes and settled back to partake of a thoroughly pedestrian meal at which everyone seemed to be working at being cheerful.

Now, look at Stuart here. Do I reconsider the word "codependency"? I depend upon you. You depend upon me. This is fine. It's square; square means balanced. Are we square, then? Evened out? I am square with my world. When I stopped using and drinking, my own morality returned like a giant force, confounding sex. "You can't have it without love. With love, it's beautiful," my mother insisted when I was growing up.

Stuart looked so neat and orderly, serious tonight. Was he *too* orderly for me? He passed with flying colors for my father, but, then, my father didn't know that Stuart was the recycled hipster. Stuart charmed him.

My mother charmed my father over and over again, even during her terrible times, leaving anguished, touching little notes on his pillow. My mother is careful tonight. "Your father had $26 when we married," she said, "and we went up to the Catskills because he had a job as a camp counselor." She sipped champagne with the care I understood far too well. The point, my mother always said, was so long as you loved each other the money didn't matter.

I get such a charge looking over at Stuart, who could care about anything else?

A. L. Rowse's *Annotated Shakespeare* in three weighty volumes was my gift to Dore, together with a couple of verses I wrote for him. He cried. (Dore cried easily, but I didn't know it until this moment.) I was sure it wasn't the power of my verses, but I felt it might well have been the notion of a newcomer to the family taking the time to honor him while he was being ignored by a cast of thousands. I was almost in tears myself at the deep sense of pathos in the occasion, the crushing descent from the exalted to the commonplace.

Dore's birthday dinner drifted to a close with probably more left unsaid than said. In my view, the people around the table were not grateful enough for their good fortune.

The Schary melodrama was, to me, a counterpoint to feelings aroused in me about my own family back in Yorkshire. The trigger was a recent letter from my mother, in response to some questions I'd asked her about my childhood. It set off a symposium of emotions and recollections.

Poverty, Stuart, is to blame for a lot of things in all our lives. When Dad got a job and off the dole, I realize you have to be a strong man not to go and get drunk when you finally have some money in your hands.

There was a whole lot more, but I couldn't deal with it all at once and, ritually, I immediately wrote a check to send to my parents. Perhaps this was why I couldn't concentrate on writing.

Sixteen

Love works when there's a balance between self-esteem and humility. Right now I was finding my self-esteem in cooking in my own house.

I called my house Topanga because Stonybrook looked like my favorite L.A. canyon. The minute I saw the house, I knew I'd be here the rest of my life. There was one main room, like an old ranch house, with an open kitchen at one end and low beams around which I'd wound ivy and wild vines.

Was I making this dinner irresistible so Stuart fell in love with my house and didn't notice how many people were here? Slivers of lemon and ginger in the cranberry sauce. Would juniper berries be amazing in the stuffing, traces of wild rice? Maybe scratch the Tex-Mex stuffing this year; chestnut stuffing is more European.

"Do you actually do Thanksgiving?" asked Jill.

I parked by the heaps of pumpkins set in big beds of straw outside the market.

"Isn't it about Pilgrims escaping England?" she asked.

"I see a Harvest Festival element in the holiday," I said. "And yes, I celebrate Thanksgiving, *and* July Fourth. You know, I did become an American citizen as soon I could and, as they say, there's no one more faithful than the converted. Besides, maybe once Thanksgiving was all about Pilgrim Fathers landing on Plymouth Rock, but the Spanish were in North America at least a hundred years earlier, Vikings long before that, and, conceivably, people from Siberia a thousand or more years before."

"Thanks." She leaned over and kissed me. "I see it just as a feast of gratitude." She was impatient with education, attending to her list. "Why do I write it down? I can spin through the market with my shopping cart and get everything I need—chestnuts, turkey, farmer's bread, cranberries, lady apples, rutabagas, celery, almonds, onions, oranges, suet for the birds and bones for the dog." She was waiting for the apple and pumpkin pies she'd ordered. Her guest list was on the same page. "Only seventeen of us this year, a small group. My parents, the children, and people who have nowhere else to go."

"I know," I said, "your house is kind of a hangout for a lot of people. So I'm not surprised they'll be here tomorrow."

"Am I doing sort of a Boys Town event to show my father I have character?" Jill said. She lifted some jugs of apple juice into our shopping cart, opened one, and drank out of it.

"I hate when you do that," I told her.

"I know, but it's how I am."

"It isn't how you have to be."

"Talking of character?"

"Something like that," I said. I nodded and smiled at a woman across the aisle. Jill stood close to me and beamed romantic triumph.

When we got to the car I put everything inside. I was still considering Thanksgiving. "Deep down it's almost a 'thank you America for taking us in' sort of occasion, and that's what should bring us all together and bring our families together. So perhaps we'll all get along in harmony tomorrow."

"Fat chance," chimed in Johanna, smiling at me. It was Thanksgiving morning and Johanna was in good spirits working alongside Jill, cleaning, peeling, and chopping food for the stuffings.

"You forgot the sausage for the Tex-Mex stuffing," Johanna said to Jill.

"I'm not doing it this year. My father would hate it."

"But Grandfox wouldn't eat it anyway," Johanna said.

"I still shouldn't have it in the house."

"You could use kosher hot dogs," Jeremy said, "and make it really eclectic."

Jill and Johanna were busy slivering orange peel, roasting chestnuts, making gravies, and swinging branches of autumn leaves and berries from the beams. They stretched cloths down the tables, which they decorated beautifully with pine cones, corncobs of various persuasions, baskets of nuts and bread, and cowboy bandanas for napkins.

"Give Grandfox this royal-blue one," Jill said.

As the time drew near, Jill was even more edgy and anxious, clearly driven by a need to impress her father. This was the first time I'd seen this so obvious compulsion to avoid any criticism from Dore. This, of course, was alien to me and, as it was, Dore seemed preoccupied with Jeremy, largely ignoring Johanna and Jill.

Seventeen of us sat down at the table, Jill presiding over the family end with her mother, Jeremy and her father to her left, and Johanna and I to her right. Jill's young girlfriend, Debbie, shepherded the recovering waifs and strays around the other end of the table. Jill began with an original blessing based on "Look to This Day," Dore followed with a Hebrew prayer, and I led the Lord's Prayer.

Dinner was superb; turkey, gravy, mashed potatoes, sweet potatoes with marshmallows, rutabagas, a traditional sage and onion stuffing, the modified and still terrific Tex-Mex stuffing, homemade cranberry sauce, chestnut pudding, pies galore, and three kinds of ice cream from Dr. Mike's in Bethel.

Jill's mother remained pretty passive throughout the proceedings, probably because this kind of affair was déclassé for her. Dore was dismissive of a lady of his own age, who was trying very hard to get his attention by praising his films and plays. I got the impression that he had little time for "nobodies." Dore also struck me as being resentful that Jill had the lead role at the party. Jeremy was of the same persuasion, taking over the prestige job of turkey carving, coached by an adoring grandfather. And then, I asked myself, 'Am I being too judgemental because I'm in a minority here and feeling like the outsider?'

After dinner, Stuart left with some of the guys to go to a men's meeting. Johanna and I started to clean up. She wanted to avoid her grandfather's teasing, which I tried to see as something he did when he felt uncomfortable, out of his territory. Johanna and Jeremy understood that their grandfather needed to be the center of attention wherever he was. Would that I could just give him that.

I grew up knowing there were some people whose talent needed reassurance. My brother and sister and I glowed with my parents' triumphs, and despaired over their failures. I am one of those needy people, too, and my children have sensed this from their rockiest early days.

My father was irritated, and my mother was furious with me for seating him next to an older woman. "What he sees here is a group of kids who don't know his work," my mother said, "and the only person in the room who does know who he is is an old woman."

Maybe I liked to entertain like this, to have my family around with a lot of other people, so I'd keep busy, performing in a way, admired for the food, the flowers, and all the theatrical distraction, so I wouldn't have to see what was really going on.

Unbelievable! When I got back to Jill's after the meeting, I found a war zone totally bereft of gratitude, a family quarrel nobody could quite decipher but somehow triggered by Dore and Jeremy.

"That is the thing with the men in our family," Jill said, glaring at Jeremy. "If it isn't their event, they'll make it theirs by letting you know what's wrong."

"Mom," Jeremy told her, "that's bullshit. You're always so crazy when Grandfox is around, and then you sat him next to that old woman he wouldn't like. You were just asking for trouble."

"Thanks, my own mother already told me that," said Jill.

"Your father is quite judgemental," I said. "He clearly favours his grandson Jeremy, even commenting on what a beautiful baby he'd been."

"My father has always dealt with his attachment to Johanna in a salty way," Jill said. "You just don't get it. He covers a lot with sarcasm."

"I usually throw it right back at him," Johanna said, "but I didn't feel like it today."

"Johanna reminds my father of his mother," Jill said, "and Johanna mistrusts sentiment. My father knows she uses an edgy wit to deal with her pain and humiliation. Don't figure out families until you've got their history."

"Like I said"—Johanna turned to me—"fat chance for us all getting together in harmony. But it was a nice try and the food was good."

Jill was in tears. I said, comforting her later, "Perhaps you were right when you said that your father has to dominate every situation."

"My father worked hard to be a leader," Jill said, "so don't expect him to just sit back and play Grandpa."

This Thanksgiving Day family experience served to reinforce a significant lesson I have learned and absorbed over the years. It is this: never, never, ever involve yourself in your partner's family disputes. These are essentially civil wars and nobody wants an outsider to be involved. Just keep out!

Seventeen

It was raining and gloomy and Monday outside. One of those days when you wake up and wish you hadn't—waking is already too much. There were just too many demands and distractions, too many problems to deal with. No wonder couples get divorced, lovers split up. Falling in love is child's play: staying in love stretches patience way beyond what one had considered to be breaking point.

Take tonight. We had been out to dinner with some acquaintances, pleasant, a little tedious, and had come home well fed and tired out. Jill, though, was suddenly sullen and fidgety, and I couldn't get her into clear focus. A woman who is feeling needy, or sexy, or sexily needy, will usually put out some signals before sliding between the sheets. But Jill was there on the bed in her panties, not talking, leafing through a magazine. This said 'not tonight' to me, and I tried to go to sleep, but this wasn't in the cards.

Jill was still sitting there, fidgeting, rubbing lotion on her body. Then, without knowing why, all hell broke loose, and we were screaming at each other. I was really angry, feeling goaded into shouting things I shouldn't. Jill was selfish and this hurtled across my adrenaline vision.

"All the bloody problems we get involved with are Jill's problems! Your father, your mother, your sick daughter, your wild son, your ex-spouses, your bloody magazine pieces, your asthma, your book, everything!" I was feeling enraged and very, very sorry for myself.

She fled into the spare bedroom and I pursued her, threw her onto the bed, tore off her panties, and made love to her. No. Wrong. I didn't make love to her or for me. I fucked her. And then I fucked her again; the defiant animal fucking that says 'you wanted fucking, how's this for size' or 'maybe this will get you off my back.' "Banging" is probably a better word, and it is a sort of transmuted violence. Rape in disguise.

And yet, in its rough, primitive way, the banging brought us both to our senses and we lay there on our backs, eyes open, holding hands, saying we were sorry and how much we loved each other.

The telephone rang, a call from Switzerland. It was Danielle, my first passionate love. She'd sent me some love letters I had written years ago, and wanted to know how I felt about them.

"Fine," I said, "but I doubt that's why you're calling me." I watched Jill carefully, fearing another bad scene.

"I'm seriously considering publishing the letters myself, here in Switzerland. Postwar youth and all that kind of stuff."

"What's really the matter, Danielle?"

"It's my husband," she said, suddenly fragile and tender. "He's acting crazy, probably having an affair, staying away on his travels much more than he used to."

"I'm really sorry, Dani," I said, "but I can't think of any way to be helpful except pray for you. I'm getting married again myself in a few months."

"Thank you, Stu. Good-bye." I heard her slam the phone down.

"I think Danielle's marriage is on the rocks," I said to Jill. "And I'm sorry about that. She fell in love with a wealthy, handsome guy, but, as we know, wealth doesn't guarantee a marriage made in heaven."

"So she's after you again," Jill said.

"I'm spoken for," I said firmly. I needed some space.

I have always loved the seaside. At first all I see is beach and water, a generic impression, like this is a meadow or a forest, but then the mind and the vision come together and deconstruct the scene. Oh yes, over there are the seagulls; and what is that patch-work of black and white on the sandbar? A covey of birds with white heads and black bodies and puffed-out breasts. Could these birds be puffins? I decide that they will indeed be puffins for me.

I'm diverted by a gull. It appears out of nowhere, flutters up and away heading into the wind coming in from Long Island Sound. It slows, becomes entirely still for a moment at its apogee, then slowly sinks down and backward to exactly the space it took off from. The bird repeats this manoeuvre time and time again. I wonder, is the gull engaged in some kind of testing procedure, or a kind of meteorological evaluation—wind speed, drift, and all that stuff I remember from my R.A.F. days.

And then it suddenly hits me. I am being far too complicated, too analytical, too unromantic. The seagull is simply playing!

That's all; just blowing in the wind, feeling the erotic caress of air over feathers, that perfect caress that needs no response, just the joy of it now and pure.

What is this all about? I ask myself. Do I want to be that bird, solo flying, playing in the ocean breeze? Am I ready for a constant companion, her family, her friends, her own needs? I realize that I'm having second thoughts about my engagement to Jill, or even, beyond that, any permanent combination. Wouldn't I have a more fulfilling life making my own way, answering only to myself, finding occasional companionship when I felt like it? Shouldn't I turn my back on being a provider and simply do what I want to do, and to hell with the consequences?

I told Trenton I was getting cold feet about my engagement and the marriage, and all the family complications on top of a new business assignment.

"Totally natural," he said, "and probably alcoholic. You want the romance *and* your own space. It doesn't have to be one or the other. When you think about it, that's how life goes for most guys most of the time. You go to work; you go home to your wife. It may be a bit tougher if you're working at home, so you have to make your own times and spaces—just like you did by being on the beach today. You're going to be okay. See ya later."

Trenton, of course, was absolutely on target. Balance was the answer, and a willingness to keep trying, to go the extra mile, and then another extra mile, and another. Loving now felt like T. S. Eliot's description of writing: "Another raid on the inarticulate, with shabby equipment deteriorating in the general mess of imprecision of feeling."

Eighteen

~

It's beginning to snow on our way down the Merritt for Barbara Goldsmith's New Year's Day party. This is our first New Year's party together. I say "party" here, because to me New Year's is always about parties—being at the best parties, and getting the most attention there. Stuart would probably be quite pleased to be alone with me, making love and resolutions. My first resolution is to have a very good time, or not to let him see if I'm cross if I'm not the center of attention.

When my sister and I went to parties, Joy would come home talking about what a great time she'd had. I would come home furious. I never got enough attention. If I wasn't the most popular person, then at least the most popular one had to like me best. Popularity was preteen fame.

I approach parties with a wary edge. No party can give me what I need, but Stuart doesn't know this yet. I thought when I met someone who really loved me back, then fame wouldn't matter. Didn't you want attention and fame so you'd feel safe and loved? Isn't Stuart's love enough?

Stuart arrives at the party so sure of himself, all stylish authority. He is totally at the party, discussing everyone's plays, films, not thinking, 'do they like what I'm wearing?'

Are Lois Gould and I going to talk tonight? No one slices lines finer, faster than Lois. She was famous first for *Such Good Friends,* the novel about the woman who finds out after her husband dies that all her consoling friends had been actually sleeping with him. Will I go over to her first? I look at her, that's how it has to be. Cut it out, I tell myself. After all, she's talking to my friend Sherman Yellen, the playwright.

We had been invited to celebrate New Year's in Manhattan at Barbara Goldsmith's and Frank Perry's place, and felt at home right away, as we arrived at the same moment as Lynn Nesbit and Dick Gilman.

I said to Dick, "This looks so different from the business world parties I'm used to. Grey flannel suits and *Wall Street Journal* chatter, as opposed to quirky costume and artsy talk."

"It's different from the academic world, too," Dick said, "but Lynn's in her element, and Jill seems to love it. They're both working the room already like mad."

I watched Jill performing. First, she concentrated on Lois Gould, a novelist she adored. They'd had some past misunderstanding, like a lover's tiff, and now they appeared to be making up. Then Jill plunged into a bunch of men writers—including Kurt Vonnegut and Tom Wolfe—who were joining in Gael Greene's inquisition of Gay Talese on his forthcoming sex epic,

Thy Neighbor's Wife. She was advancing a strong viewpoint in the midst of a male barrage of sexual and ribald cliches.

"I think you're both from northern England," said Frank Perry, introducing me to Albert Finney.

"Yorkshire," I said, "white rose county."

"Lancashire," Finney said, "red rose county."

"So let's not have the War of the Roses," said Frank. "Be friendly."

"No problem," I said. "We were all in the same boat up north. When I saw Albert Finney in *Saturday Night and Sunday Morning,* I wanted to yell out, 'that's my story,' that was my world."

"Postwar Britain," said Finney. "Youth disillusionment after a war they thought would change the dreary working-class lives, and nothing changed."

"Which is why we had that generation of Angry Young Men, as they became known," I said. "And why I decided to leave it all behind and come to America."

"And didn't do so badly, I'd guess," said Finney, looking around the room.

"Not bad," I said, "but not a star, like you. I've been in the business world for a few years and that's a different cast of characters, different successes, all about money."

As we drifted to other conversations, I felt the pangs of this encounter with Finney, the stark memories of an exhausted England, and the driving urge to escape and to create something, and to be somebody. And here I am, surrounded by real talent, not just celebrity. What talent do I have? How do I compare with these bright stars, these writers and artists, Larry Rivers, Jacques d'Amboise, Robert Benton? Self-pity rears its mushy head.

"And what do you do?" the commanding woman standing before me asked. "I'm Irene Selznick, hello."

"Very little compared to the things you've done," I said, "especially your work with Tennessee Williams. As a matter of fact, when you said 'hello,' I was just asking myself what did I do, what have I done, all that envious stuff, and beginning to feel very unaccomplished."

"Who are you with?" Irene said.

"I'm with Jill Robinson, and we're engaged to be married this year."

"Well then, life is full of promise for you already. I know Jill and she wrote a powerful story about love and alcoholism, and with a powerful woman beside you, you're already ahead of the game. If you're really in love, you're in a very select company. Look around," she said with a smile.

Stuart has lost himself in Irene Selznick's ravenous, dazzling presence, exchanging lines of poetry and plays with her as easily as he'd dusted off the snowflakes from his jacket on the way in tonight. I see what had knocked over every woman he's ever met, from the elegant Danielle to the perfectly British Margaret, to me. Here is Stuart, the way he must have been as a student, all eager rapture. Irene is all sophisticated wit; Stuart, the young man with the older woman who owns the world he really wants. Can I captivate him long enough? Do I have the diligence for the intellectual push-ups he will require? Can I actually be interested in serious music? Can I miss a summer in the Hamptons so he can show me Europe?

Stuart's English accent always plays well, adding substance to my quirky L.A. twang. Smart couples know the deals they've made. Some deals involve property, ambition, and money, which can, with compatible wit and guest lists, look a lot like love.

I feel the shift in my spirits. I am watching Dominick Dunne talking with Brooke Hayward. Brooke, who is either in despair, or joyful and feeling superior. Tonight I can't tell yet.

There are instants, like a frame here and there in a long trail of film, where I see the grin, the rosy cheeks and fresh joy I saw in Brooke all the time when we were growing up, playing with the giant dollhouse in their barn, or tearing around the lawn, trying to see who could run faster and swing higher. All that mattered very much then. But five years later, what mattered most was who had asked you out, and would you be allowed to wear strapless. Then Brooke was on the cover of *Life*, for which the fame furies would never forgive her.

Do you know when you have a "deal"? Do we have one or are we simply in love? A blissful connection of souls—do I believe in that? And can that master real life? Is working reality the affliction that collapses some marriages? Were we just complicating sex here? Was sex best not tangled up with love's responsibilities and, I thought, my family?

Was this a little late to ask such questions? How long are you together before you stopped wondering if it really was a great idea after all? Do you ever stop, or do you get to a point at which you say, 'we're married, we were smart when we did that.' You have days when you hate yourself, and you don't say, 'I think I'll just leave.' So I told myself, 'shut up and get on with it.'

Love. I looked around, considering how so many friends here have defined and explored and rejected it. For sure, love is the uncool addiction, and here I am doing it again. This romantic notion of a spiritual attachment, this kind of love we claim comes in late on the list of priorities for some of us. Will it fit in the elevator? Does it travel?

We're leaving early, it's a long ride home. I hate to be the first to go.

Later, as Irene Selznick was leaving, she took my arm. "It's good to see you and Jill together. I've been watching you and you are a strong man. You will be good for each other."

We drive home through a blinding snowstorm, leaving behind the sweet smell of success, and I half listen to Jill as I contemplate our future and try to stay on the road.

Then, I can't explain it. Suddenly, making a pot of tea together in the kitchen, the mood changed. There probably wasn't any rational reason for the blow-up. One moment we were singing "Lonesome Polecat" from *Seven Brides* and talking about her dad's picture and trying to remember cast names. Then she was furious that she wasn't a "real famous writer" like Vonnegut, Wolfe, and all, and how she'd thrown away her life. All hell broke loose.

"What a selfish, lousy, rotten way to finish a glorious day," I yelled at her.

"So, go home and get out of my life!" she screamed, and flung a pile of books across the room. She stalked off through the deep snow to her writing studio behind the house.

I now wanted to kill her, or at least beat some sense into her. My time of sobriety was slipping through my fingers like good intentions saying 'fuck you.' My old primitive self was screaming to come back into a lead role. 'Let me do some damage' was the message I was receiving loud and clear.

Then a shaft of sanity penetrated my brain. I recalled a conversation with Trenton after Jill and I had an argument one day on Southport's main street.

I'd got into my Jeep and headed out of town, going hell-for-leather anywhere, nowhere. But I stopped and called Trenton from a phone in the diner. I gabbled out my story to Trenton, about how Jill had said this, that, and the other. Silence on the phone. I start to gabble again.

Then Trenton said, "Shut the fuck up."

"What kind of advice is that?" Silence.

"Shut the fuck up. Listen. Just answer me one question. Do you want to marry this girl or not?"

"Yes, Trenton, but . . ."

"Shut the fuck up. If you love this girl enough to want to marry her, you've got to change your attitude. When you're mad as hell, always—and I mean always—do the exact opposite of what you feel like doing. Instead of beating the shit out of someone, you be nice, you apologize or whatever."

So, here I was wanting to be violent, and there she was in the studio, twenty-five yards away through the snow, and all I could think of was Trenton's advice. Trenton, you bastard!

I slammed the door to my house and stood on the porch. He didn't follow. The snow was falling. I remembered a story where the lovers fight in the snow. He makes snowballs and throws them at her, and instead of running into the house, she runs around the house and finally falls down. Her lover wonders whether he'll help her up or kick more snow over her.

I'd like to shout at Stuart, get him out here and throw snowballs at him, but I forget who I'm dealing with. Stuart retreats when he fights in order to save my life. I'd started the fight, and now I had to live with it.

I peeled off all my clothes until I was stark naked, barefoot. I marched through the calf-deep snow to Jill's studio. I threw open the door, strode in, fixed my eyes on a frightened Jill and said, "Let's make love. Now!"

So after all, this had been a wonderful way to start the New Year, the year in which we were to become husband and wife, forever.

Nineteen

Stuart was the first man I'd ever been in love with who had my father's kind of presence. Stuart spoke and people listened, the way people always listened when my father spoke. Stuart had the style; he moved into formality with the same suave charm. I guess presence comes with an early appreciation of your talent, and then the tricky achievement of authority without arrogance.

Stuart caught very quickly my obsession with my family, especially my attachment to my father. He told me very early that he'd never seen anything quite like it. And as I watched Stuart and my father, I could feel the pull inside myself. Which one would I turn to? Which one needed me today?

What I probably most admired about my future father-in-law was his resilience. Dore Schary was the comeback kid to me and my everlasting mentor in that regard. I see him now in the upstairs room at Sardi's, making a pitch to "angels" for backing of his next project, a big-time, Western musical. Steve Carmen belting out the songs, Dore at the podium telling the story, his voice weak but his stance upright and dramatized by his cowboy outfit.

When we'd gone down to visit him shortly after the Sardi's reading just before Christmas 1979, his situation had not sounded good. Miriam's pessimism was in stark contrast to Dore's optimistic attitude, but probably nearer to the reality of affairs. She pulled me aside and whispered, "Dore's illness could be critical." I had the sense that Miriam, by contemplating the worst outcome, would find the slightest relief to be a miracle.

My father had called this morning and asked if I'd like to come down to the city and be with him in the afternoon. He was going to be on the Dick Cavett show. "Absolutely," I said.

They sent a limo for him, and as we sat in the stillness, he put his hand on mine. I hoped for a traffic jam so we'd have more of this time.

"I wanted some time to talk to you," he said.

"I figured that," I said quickly. "This reminds me of when you'd ask me to come along with you to the studio in the morning after I'd left a story for you to read on your pillow."

"Sometimes we'd just go for a ride up the coast," he said.

"Or around the canyons. You'd wear an old sweater and not slick your hair back. We'd drive and drive and talk about writing. Or you'd be thinking and I'd be quiet." I reached over and clasped my hands around his. "You've got something hard to tell me."

We were jammed up at a light going crosstown. We could've been in any canyon, walled in by buildings.

"They've found cancer, Jill, that they can't fix." He shook his head.

"Foxxie, no." We'd talked about him dying before. He'd been sick so often. "You know it will be all right."

"No, it won't. I'm not going to let them tear me apart. I want you to understand that. Your mother does.

"I do." It was different now. "How long do you think you have?"

"A couple of months."

The limousine was the perfect set for this. Silent, soft, removed, the way you guess death might be, where you'll be able to see what's going on but they can't see you. You can't connect.

My father and I spent a lot of time that afternoon talking about my kids. "Johanna's going to be all right," he told me, "she has my mother's strength." But my father was Jeremy's mentor. "Jeremy will miss me most of all. Watching him is like watching myself, and he's going through troubled times, feeling adrift the way I did when I was a kid after my father left. It's easier if you feel needed. My mother needed me. He'll listen to Stuart because Stuart's smart, but Stuart won't be able to be a father to him."

Jeremy never accepted any other man I'd put in place of his own father. His grandfather was his role model for achievement, leadership, a complex figure projecting warmth and distance.

After dinner in the city, Jill and I drove home, slowly and carefully in a pouring rain. I felt a profound sense of an old order giving way to the new, of liaisons forming and re-forming. It was hard to resist the idea of *la forza del destino* when the fragments, so jagged and irregular, as if by some mystical signal smooth themselves into satisfying geometrics.

So many shards in the dark night. The prospect of death and marriage, taking Jill's father's place as well as my own with her. Lucrative employment and how will that get in the way of my writing. What was to become of us? What commitments were truly and firmly made? What was real?

The rain pelted the Jeep and the slipping tires on the wet road were like the crosscurrents of my emotions, powerful and unpredictable. What is an honest emotion? How will I recognize it? Doubt is a curse. My vision must be circumscribed so that I may see only one truth at a time, deal with it and then move forward.

Hurry up, please, it's time.
Hurry up, please, it's time.

When my father told me he was dying, the God I was aware of was the Old Jewish God you could have these talks with. He looked like Eli Wallach (on good days, like my father long ago), His hands on His hips. "So, where have you been?"

"We'll talk about that later," I said.

"Get to the point," He said, "I've got a heavy day."

"This isn't a big deal in the scheme of things, not life and death, but can I get married in a church when my father's dying?"

"This may surprise you, but, frankly, your wedding is the last thing on your father's mind right now. Try and think about that for a minute. Somebody's waiting and there's another call coming in."

This is why I usually pray to trees, to shelves of books I love, and to the images of old canyons. But then, God knows.

It is the best of times: it is the worst of times. I mean those few weeks before the wedding. Jill was getting panicky, particularly with the combination of Johanna moving out to her own apartment, away from Jill's nest, and the unnecessarily complex wedding arrangements. I felt helpless in this situation, and it bothered me. I recognised that Johanna and Jill had been together for so many years, with Johanna sometimes assuming the role of mother, but I sensed that the best support I could give them both was to take a backseat and let the separation evolve as it may.

Then, of course, there was the challenge of Jill's parents. I was to meet Jill at her parents' apartment after an appointment. I walked through the endless theater of Central Park on a balmy afternoon. It was sunny softball games, long-legged girls, gaggles of joggers, cyclists, blossoms sprinkled on the pond's sheen surface, a silver-haired man in old formal dress staring at a *New York Times*. And my mind pictured Dore.

At teatime, I presented myself at the Scharys' apartment. Dore appeared in a robe, unsteady on his feet, and when I embraced him, he felt like a bony whippet starved for racing at a Yorkshire miners' dog track. No, he was more like my sister, Marjorie, who had a terrible kidney ailment that saw her alternatively grossly bloated or emaciatedly thin. This was during the war when I was the teenage man of the house. Dreadful air-raid nights when I had to carry Marjorie down the stairs to shelter under a kitchen table, the proper air-raid shelter being too cold and damp for my sick sister. When she was swollen she was quite heavy, and I rather guiltily found myself praying for her to be skinny during the air-raid nights.

Dore struck me now as hungry for the spirit from contact. He relished our visit and an earlier call on him by John Lindsay, seeking advice from a respected Jewish leader for his senatorial race. I understood this: to feel necessary is to feel alive. We chatted about writing, and I wondered if a creative endeavor can actually reinforce the will to live. We discussed the idea.

"I'm sure that, ultimately, loving and being loved, the way it is with you and Miriam, and with Jill and me, helps prolong our lives."

"Life insurance studies prove that," Dore said. "Loving couples live years longer than less fortunate people."

"Yes, that's true, but beyond that, I believe Jill will extend my life by her interestingness."

"You mean get more out of your days, as I have with Miriam."

"Exactly. Jill italicizes my days. She makes them more memorable, and therefore, more abundantly lived."

"I like that," said Dore, "*italicizes my days.*"

"As opposed to blandness," I said, "which is instantly forgettable. It shortens our experience of life, for life is measured not so much by calendars or clocks, but by experiences and events."

"And, Lord knows, Miriam and I have had a goodly share of dramatic events and varied experiences."

Dore was tired out by the conversation, but remained in good spirits. I sensed that he had his mind set on enduring at least through our wedding, six weeks from now. Oh my God! Are we even thinking of days and weeks now?

I was convinced from my reading of his character that Dore would plan his own exit. It would be a dignified one, not a slow, dragging shuffle off the stage, full of masking medications and enfeebled gestures. No. He would want to stride off, pausing in the wings for a final turn to the audience and his last straight look at them before a final smile and a wave of the hand. A salute.

I felt my father had already given up the battle. He'd fought enough, and my mother had no fire left to give him.

I looked at Stuart. I could not let him see how desperate this made me, how much my father meant. Stuart must be everything to me now. This was the deal. Our spiritual life first, and then each other. There was no, 'but once in a while someone else. . . .' I could not let this fear get in here now, could not let grief put its feet in the door of this marriage. I didn't have to tell my father that I'd found my own man. He knew.

Twenty

~

I didn't like his bed, the kind that comes from a freeway shop the size of Monrovia. Stuart had turned on his side with his hands under his chin, as if he were praying. He moved one arm now, back, and touched me, stroked my arm down from my shoulder.

"Down," he was saying, "down." He shifted his torso, backing into me, fixing himself here snugly, and the bed creaked. You would not expect this bed to creak.

I wanted to get up after he fell asleep. Do women ever rest? Do I remember a sleep when I wake up surprised to see morning has arrived? Was this the mother, always on guard? Are they breathing?

I called Johanna. We could have breakfast, walk on the beach, sit shoulder by shoulder, and she'd feel I'm here for her.

I made coffee for Stuart to have when he woke up, then drove home and got there just as Johanna was pulling up. A completely unattractive picture of late-twentieth-century American values. There's this house, this image of quaint domestic serenity, but the mother and daughter have each spent the night somewhere else.

"I called last night," she said, "but you were at his house, so I stayed at Tracy's." She put bagels in the toaster.

"Really?" I was suspicious.

"Really," she said. "I'm seeing Dr. Bailey after school today." Dr. Bailey was Reilly's vet. "I'm going to work for him and get training references to be a vet." Reilly came over when he heard the vet's name. "No, you're not going," and Johanna gave him a biscuit.

"You're tense and angry with me," I said.

"No," she said, "you are with me, and it's not because of anything we should be fighting about."

"Like you've been out all night."

"So have you," she said.

"But you knew where I was."

"And you knew where I was."

"Sort of. You know, you haven't called your grandfather all week."

"But when I do he teases me, and I don't feel like that now. Anything else?"

"You're not working on your photography, and suddenly you announce you're taking a job with a vet without even talking about it."

"I want a real job." She buttered the bagels while I put honey in the tea.

"Johanna, my father always told me that the thing that would save my life is my writing, and your talent is photography. You just turn your back on yourself when you desert it. You know your grandfather says the most important thing is initiative."

"I thought you said it was talent." She narrowed her eyes. "Maybe you ought to check with him."

"Johanna, how can I ever get anything right with you? Look, I used to get involved in political things when I had an article to finish. You remember. It was hard to stick with one thing."

"Thanks for the advice," she said, "I mean it." She went along with what I was saying to get out of here again, which was exactly what I would have done. "I'll go take a few pictures right now." She snapped herself into her down coat, whipped her scarf round her neck, and stomped out to her car.

"I shouldn't have been so tough with Johanna," I told Stuart when he picked me up later to go to a meeting.

"I'm sure you weren't," he said. "You were doing what a mother does. You were taking responsibility."

"But I don't want to be that kind of mother."

"If you weren't, you'd feel guilty about that."

I looked at his profile in the glaring light set against the dark pines you could see through the car's big windows. I studied the eyebrows, the hair, the square jaw, and I wondered—since he wasn't really interested in kids, hated my house and the way I loved to keep it full of people and food and noise and didn't mind about it being messy, didn't like some of my friends, hated the Village and the music I liked—what were we doing here? And he liked to travel, and I would not do that.

I would have to go to England to meet his parents, but that's the honeymoon, no more than a week. I couldn't imagine people who just took off, leaving their kids and houses for weeks, even months. My parents went to Europe—once—and took my brother and sister. I was already married. It was hard enough to leave L.A. for the East Coast. My parents were here, my work is here, but to leave my own land, the ocean, trees, my territory? Never.

Tears. "Could we pull over so I can call Johanna?"

"Jill, let go of it."

"It's not that simple. Some kids won't even see their parents, they just stop talking to them. I'd hate that."

"And there are people who won't stop talking about their children—and people who hate that," he said, his brow stormy, lowering, like thunder.

"You don't get it, do you? How much they mean to me?"

"I'm beginning to." He got that warning look. He put his hand on my knee.

"Are you all about sex?" Was that really what was breaking up the neat triangle of my kids and me?

"No," he said, "but you're all about writing. At least one of us remembers what Gloria said. You've got a deadline. That's what's really bothering you. After the meeting, I'm taking you home to write."

He was right. The best thing I can do for this marriage will be to write—keep myself occupied, keep my spirit absorbed in my own days. Writing was my garden. I dug around in the pages, tore out old dead roots, finding fresh seeds, planting them neat so they'll grow straight along well-weeded paths.

Twenty-One

 ~

There is a shade of light blue suffused with yellow that belongs to April and announces the romance of spring. The scene resembles those photographs of blue objects in which some distortion has tinged the peripheries of the blues with amber, as with light piercing pendant prisms dangling from glossy chandeliers, or those blue and yellow marbles too precious to play with in the gutters. So are we, Jill and I, suffused with spring on this bright April morning. What a day to start thinking about our wedding on Midsummer's Day, not quite three months away!

We showed up for the early morning meeting and stayed behind to talk to Ted Hoskins about the possibility of getting married in his church. Ted showed us into his cluttered office, making us feel instantly at home. He never gave you the impression he's too busy to see you. No wonder his congregation adored him.

"What can I do for you two lovely people?" he asked. We could not have pictured a more appropriate man as our wedding minister. Straight from central casting, Ted was bluff and bearded, twinkle-eyed mischief and kindness, and full of his God and his church.

"We'd like you to marry us in your church," Jill said quickly, "but I guess that's a problem because I'm Jewish."

"And I'm Church of England," I added, and began to outline the issues that could cause trouble; the previous marriages, Christian and Jewish, formal education and very little schooling, a Yorkshire mining town boy and a Hollywood princess. "How do we reconcile that mix in a marriage?" I asked.

"And we both have kids from prior marriages," Jill said.

"Whoa," Ted said—bellowed, rather—"as far as religion goes, that can be quite simple. There is only one God." And at that moment, everything became terribly simple for Jill and for me.

Reassured by the simplicity of his approach to religion, we talked to him about a marriage ceremony. Jill was surprised and delighted with the sweet reasonableness of Hoskins and how smoothly and expeditiously all the church arrangements were set. When we left Ted's office it was all done and dusted. We would be married at noon on Saturday, June 21, 1980.

Later in the day we looked at wedding invitations at a shop in Westport, and Jill was attracted to a white, frilly dress at Laura Ashley; "It looks like a pioneer woman's dress," she said. Then to top it off we ran into Martha Stewart. After listening to Jill's story of the Ted Hoskins meeting, Martha said, "Okay. Listen, if you'll provide the food and let me take pictures for my book on entertaining, I'll arrange the whole reception for you." Ecstatic agreement by both of us.

"As it is," I said to Jill on the drive home, "since this is an interdenominational wedding and since we spend so much time at Gold's Delicatessen, we'll have Julius Gold do some of the food."

"Yes." Jill laughed. "Martha and Julius, interdenominational food!"

That night my friends Susan and Don Granger arrived early for a dinner party. A brunette with a big smile, Susan grew up in L.A. While Stuart and Don talked, Susan helped me put dinner together. Like a doubles tennis match, she darted back and forth to the table, I chopped shallots, she slipped tortillas into the oven; I tossed salad, she sliced bread; flip this, whip that.

Susan and Don had separated a while ago, and it had been a phenomenal shock. They had the perfect marriage: Don, a successful, forceful, very conservative neurologist; Susan an entertaining writer and broadcast journalist who genuinely loves Hollywood. We were all relieved when they got back together. I knew they'd be one of the couples we'd want to entertain, right here, for the rest of our lives.

When we finally lit the candles and sat down to dinner with Gerry and Franca Mulligan and Brooke Hayward and Peter Duchin, I was delighted. Their faces glowed in this rustic scene, with the wooden beams and the shingled walls. You wanted to be with couples who took turns comforting each other during dark times; couples who understood each other's mythic images, keeping the good ones going and the bad ones out.

Brooke and Peter had a romantic insight into each other, a tender understanding of their difficult childhoods and the early loss of parents. She felt sheltered enough and loved him enough to give the impression she was amused most of the time. Peter had the great cheer and fast humor Brooke needed. Gerry and Franca Mulligan were tall, lean figures, Gerry's silver-blue eyes and snow-white beard glacial next to Franca's gorgeous dark Italian looks. Franca sheltered Gerry, the way I wanted Stuart to protect me.

Curiously, the subject of houses came up.

"A man wants the house he owns, a house he has found himself," Franca said with regal authority.

"Maybe," I said, "Stuart will have a sense of belonging when he brings his own things into our house."

"It's not *our* house." Stuart made it very clear that this house would never be his house.

"But once you hang your pictures," I said, "fix things the way you want." I knew this was a losing battle.

"Stuart doesn't fix things." Peter laughed. "I could tell you that."

"Nothing *can* be fixed," Stuart said. "It's an important consideration about a house in Connecticut. You can't find experts to come right over—the roads will be frozen or their truck will be in the shop."

Susan didn't mince words. "I took one look at Stuart, and I knew you cannot have *that* man living in *this* house," she said, and she smiled at Stuart. "You can see how a man really wants to live by really looking at what he has around him. Look at his desk, no clutter. That's what he wants. Women are much more adaptable, so adapt. You'll both be much happier."

"There is a contemporary house on the water near us that would be perfect for Stuart," Franca said.

"I'd feel like I was on display in such a house," I said. "You have to keep everything neat every minute."

"That's the point," said Don.

"Our friend Toby lives in California," Brooke said, "and Tom, the man she loves, lives in New York. Maybe that's an option."

"Actually, Brooke and I saw a wonderful house yesterday," I said, as I brought out the dessert, "a big turn-of-the-century house, but with all that ivy and the deep porches all around, Stuart will hate it."

Franca gave him her grand protective look. "I hate it already," Stuart said.

Twenty-Two

~

We were visiting Ted Hoskins to talk about our future together, the meaning of marriage and the priorities of married life.

"The most important observation I've made since I've known you," said Ted, "is that you're obviously deeply in love, and you are highly motivated to make your relationship, your coming marriage, work. This meeting is an obvious sign of that willingness to work at it and fix it as necessary or desirable. So let's talk about priorities. What do you think is your paramount priority, Jill?"

"I would have thought my family," said Jill, "until I met Stuart, and now I feel he may be at the top of the list."

"And you, Stuart?"

"No question. I'd put Jill as my top priority."

"Okay," said Ted, "let's discuss that for a while. It strikes me that both of you, via your addictions, had some very troubled times, almost lethal situations. In fact, both of you are lucky to be alive. Yet during those times, you each had a lover as a priority.

Certainly your own welfare didn't appear to rate that highly with you. Then you found sobriety, or it found you, and presumably with the help of your God, some higher power, you were able to get your lives back on track. Does this suggest anything to you about your priorities?"

"Well, I can't be a reliable, stable partner, capable of exchanging strong ideas and support, if I lose my connection to the program. That's got to come first for me," said Jill.

"Right, Ted," I said, "without sobriety the rest is conversation."

"To me," said Jill, "a higher power is God, and I know that people have different ideas about that. You said when you agreed to marry us that there's only one God."

"Perhaps," said Ted, "that meant that the idea of God is big enough to encompass all the disparate visions of Him, or Her, or whatever."

"I get through a lot of this," I said, "by concentrating on what a spiritual life is rather than what God is. I know if I get through a day without telling a lie, I'm an honest man today, and if I'm an honest man today, the likelihood is that I'm living a spiritual life."

"That's pretty good," said Ted. "Any comments, Jill?"

"Well, yes. I feel that the spirit is in nature, the trees, the land, and I feel that spirits go on and on. And in some mysterious way, that there's a good spirit in my writing."

"That's pretty good, too," said Ted. "You both share a belief in a force, a power, a spirit beyond yourselves, and it doesn't matter much what names we give to that force."

Jill said, "So after sobriety as our key priority, I guess our love for each other is the second priority."

"Indeed, yes," said Ted, "and you know from your own unsuccessful experiences that that takes a lot of effort."

"To me," I said, "it means walking the extra mile toward a compromise when we have a disagreement."

"And what happens if that doesn't work?" asked Jill.

"Then I think you walk another extra mile, and another, and another, until the matter is resolved," said Ted.

"Tough," I said, "but I'll certainly make that commitment."

"Me, too," said Jill, taking my hand in hers.

"Now, perhaps I can make a suggestion," said Ted, smiling. "I think three priorities is plenty. You have two already—your spiritual life and your love for each other—so perhaps the third and final priority is 'everything else.'"

"Wow!" exclaimed Jill, "that means my writing."

"And making a living, money," I hastened to add.

"Precisely," pronounced Ted. "But you must see that in the past Jill's writing, her desire for fame, and your drive for power, money, have got you into trouble. Only if these drives are subjugated to spirituality and love will you stand a chance for the wonderful relationship you long and pray for."

"That will be tough," said Jill.

"Especially when Gloria says with Jill the priority is always the book, and with me the drive to worldly success has always been there. But I know that has screwed me up. I'm willing to accept these priorities," I say.

"There'll be times, of course," interjected Ted, "when your work or your family and children are a priority. But these priorities are really for the long haul. You don't embark on any major endeavour without assessing its potential impact on your priorities. If it looks as though the endeavour would compromise your spiritual well-being or your love for each other, then you just don't do it. Period."

Jill said, "You know, you're absolutely right, Ted. I need to see things, to do things differently."

"Yes," I said, "this time we've got to get it right."

"Well done, then," said Ted. "You're getting married by me in this church on Midsummer's Day and your priorities are your spiritual well-being, first and foremost; your love for each other, second; and, third, everything else."

The three of us agreed that these would indeed be our priorities until death do us part.

Jill and I retired to Gold's Deli for coffee and a sandwich, and a review of our session with Ted. I knew the third priority—'everything else'—wasn't going to be easy for Jill. Jill is very gregarious and I am not. Jill, in fact, would prefer virtually anybody's company than none at all, and I often prefer solitude.

"I feel we are really committed now," said Jill.

"I agree," I said, "but let's talk a bit more about the 'everything else' part, because I believe that's where the danger lurks. Everything else covers your writing, my making a living, a lot of stuff, like family and friends. And then there's money."

"Stuart," said Jill, "we'll be able to cope with money if we keep it in its priority."

"But first," I interjected, "I feel strongly that we need to air the money subject thoroughly so we know where we stand. Obviously, my situation is precarious; otherwise I wouldn't be selling the Buick and the piano. And you don't have any idea of your finances."

"That's why we're going to the city to see Professor Ziegler," said Jill, "and get things sorted out."

Twenty-Three

~

"So, how's it coming, Stu?" asked John Mehegan, my jazz buddy. "Things seem to have developed with you and Jill since that first night you introduced us at Dameon's."

"Yeah, and we don't see ya no mo'!" This was Dexter Robinson, our mutual friend. "You still got that gangsta car we bought in Saratoga after a good day with the ponies?"

"As a matter of fact, guys, things are going just fine with Jill and me, but the car has got to go."

"Too bad," said Dex, shrugging. "Remember that jaunt to the Bill Evans Memorial in Manhattan, and then how you bastards took off for Paris without me?"

"Yeah. American Express and my bank manager remember, too, which leads to why I'm selling the car, and"—I hesitated— "the grand piano."

"Sonofabitch," spat out Mehegan, "how can you let that go?"

"John, it's cold, hard reality. I'm broke. Until some consulting gigs come through, I've got to come up with some scratch."

"That breaks my heart," said Dexter.

"Money may not be the root of all evil," said John, "but it sure has a way of screwing up relationships."

"So," said Dexter, "if the car and piano have to go, they gotta go. But what about Jill, her bestseller books?"

"Dex, Jill's books have done better critically than commercially, and she's used the book money bringing up her kids. No alimony, no child support, just a talented working woman."

"So what are you going to do?" asked John.

"Well, for openers I'm going to the city to meet with Jill's accountant. That will be illuminating."

"Have a good trip," said John.

"Catch you later," said Dex.

"Is this how you're trying to show me you're watching money?" Stuart glared at me while I was getting dressed. "From the inside out?" he said, holding me around the waist, taking off the old bra and tossing it into the wastebasket. "This has got to go."

This was going to be a vile day.

Jill's accountant, Professor Ziegler, was a large, older, white-haired man. He was standing behind an ornate, bare desk, staring in our general direction. He was blind.

The receptionist announced us. "This is Jill Robinson with her fiancé, Mr. Shaw. They're here to discuss Jill's financial position as they're about to be married." She then withdrew.

The professor worked his way around his desk, holding on to

it, and felt his way to a chair. "Sit down, please." He beckoned, and rang a bell.

A Chinese woman appeared and addressed the professor in Chinese. The professor answered in Hebrew, and as the woman disappeared he confided, "Mrs. Leung is going to get your file." When Mrs. Leung returned with Jill's file, Professor Ziegler again spoke to her in Hebrew and then translated for us, "I'm asking Mrs. Leung to read us my summary of your situation."

Mrs. Leung somehow managed to wade through the summary, but all we could really determine was that, in Mrs. Leung's words, "Jill have some money before. Jill have no money now. Jill spend too much money." I blotted out the rest of this babel.

Stuart looked grim as we walked down Fifth Avenue. One thing I would be having was a new accountant.

"Stuart, I'm devastated. You shouldn't have to hear that sort of thing. It will be fine, though, I promise."

"Jill, denying the situation, hiding it from me, isn't going to make it better. Having an accountant who is blind with an assistant who doesn't speak English is a splendid metaphor for your financial condition—an inexpressible mess," he said. "We should change your accountant immediately, and we know people in Southport who will help us. You've been a giving person, perhaps to a fault, but we can do better at handling money. First, we need to agree on what we think about money."

Would we change how we were if we had a lot of money? I asked myself. Would he expect me to be all splendidly groomed, done up to a high finish every day? And if I did, would I write less and lose the vitality that turns him on? Would he become controlling? Did I mind someone taking over a part of my life I don't handle well? Did I have to handle everything? So, money is not my talent. Maybe the point is just to be honest about it.

He was being gentle with me. Most men when they talk about money cover their concern with anger. He knew I was embarrassed. How to fix it fast?

"Let's finish this discussion later," he said, and pulled me into Saks. Fourth floor, lingerie, of course.

"Something beige," I told the woman helping us. I was smiling, "We're getting married. He can't see the dress, but he can see the bra." She closed the door as she left us together in the fitting room.

I looked at myself in the three-way mirror. I stretched up. He was standing behind me. I clutched at the top of the mirror with both hands. He reached his right hand down, gripping me. "You're getting warm. I feel the connections. I hear you," he whispered.

It's not just physical. He knows. It's a spot in the psyche—and he's got it. The cell says 'yeah, that's what I'm looking for.'

"More, please." I saw myself from every angle. "Three faces, six breasts, a dozen arms and legs. I am your distracted abstraction."

He watched as I dipped my breasts into the silky smooth cups of one of the bras the woman brought in. I smartened up straight as she adjusted the straps like a fine rider with a perfect hunch for her mare's next move. She had a polished anonymous allure. Did she have her phone number on business cards for men who came in alone?

I turned and held his face between my hands, kissing his lips. "Soft, smile soft, not fierce."

He handed me the other peachy lace bra draped over the black Regency chair. "Try this."

"Anatole once said appreciating a woman's dress is almost as complicated as interpreting her dreams," I said. "So I suppose that applies to my undress?"

"An interesting complication. What you wear is the fastest way to tell how you feel. Easier than dreams."

"Which bra do I want?" I asked.

"Both." He handed the woman his credit card when she returned.

When I shop with Stuart, he becomes the gallant Continental entrepreneur. The very dash of the gesture with which he slaps his card onto the counter lengthens my legs six inches. I stand sideways to the counter, one hand on my hip, an eyebrow raised, 'see what I've got.'

"But this is exactly what we have to be careful about," I said, "to only get what we really need."

"Two bras aren't going to make the difference," he said.

The woman gave me the bag as we left, and she handed Stuart her card, "If you ever need anything," she said, then added carefully, "for your wife."

"We'll let you know," I said quickly. "I dreamed last night that I met a woman who thought she was alone until two weeks later her whole fortune changed."

"Are you sure?" She was so eager.

"Absolutely," I said.

Love is so pleasing during these intervals. "Bright intervals," Stuart calls them, like the British weather reports. During times like this, we caught people feeling so pleased for us, yet so full of longing for themselves. Love isn't a limited item, but when you've been on your own, it's hard to believe there's any left to come your way.

"Let's go to the Waldorf," he said when we're walking along the street again. "Only a few blocks. We can take a room—tea—room service."

"Oh, Stuart." I faced him, "this is exactly not the idea. We don't need to glamorize what we've got. We can just go home—you wanting me, me wanting you. It will just get stronger."

But was this the wrong place to save money? We like a little dark complexity to sex. I never wanted to use all my erotic mystery on creative cooking; never wanted to spend too much time scouting flavors to astonish him when I could better spend this time on new tricks of the older trade.

Maybe there would be a future society where cookbooks would be circulated in plain brown wrappers, and sex would be what you go out to have with a few close friends. I must be careful not to talk too much about how this works, and sometimes why not. He did not need reminders of my hang-ups and ghosts. It would be a matter of tension and timing, building the day's allure. By the time we got home, the longing was stronger still.

Don't open the mail. Don't pick up the messages. Go directly to bed. Yes.

The next day we had our money talk.

"We can deal with money like our Viking oath," Jill said. "You promised 'to love and protect' me and I promised 'to hear you and to love you.' So, you'll handle money in a protective way—and I'll listen to your advice."

"That's a good preamble," I said. "I agree completely. Now let's get specific about the topic—money."

"I've never cared all that much about money," Jill said. "It's the fame I've been chasing."

"And I've never cared all that much about money either," I said. "It's the power I've been seeking. So, if money isn't our priority, perhaps it will be easy for us to agree that we just put everything into a common pot and take out what we need, with both of us agreeing to any major purchase. Shall we say anything over five hundred dollars?"

"I'll buy that," Jill said, "and we'll probably talk over spending even smaller amounts than that."

We talked into the night about money, savings, needs, and desires. Perhaps the most important part of this was our ability to deal with it in an honest, open manner. We built a climate of trust where neither of us would think about spending money without talking to the other.

Twenty-Four

I was talking about my upcoming honeymoon with Jack, an old drinking buddy of mine. "Hey," Jack smarted, "I'm an expert. I've had three honeymoons, and they were all funerals for the marriages."

"Jesus, Jack, what went wrong?"

"A lot of things. First, I'd tell any guy to sort out the sex subject before the honeymoon. I lost my first wife the first night. 'Too fast, too selfish, too rough'—the divorce in six words."

"So, it's a good idea to sort out sexual compatibility ahead of time," I said. "I think we've done that. What happened to the second bride?"

"You won't believe this, Stu, and I'll spare you the details, but this honeymoon fell apart because she couldn't share a bathroom with a man, and we had to take a second room for her. We were never close after that."

"So, you should have got it together the third time, Jack, right?"

"I thought I had, Stu, but the third lady had a 'class' problem. She hated museums and art galleries, which I'd overlooked during a lightning courtship. My mistake. We're in New York, I go to the Guggenheim, she goes to Barney's. We're in Paris, I go to the Louvre, she goes to a boutique. She's a damn shopaholic, Stu. Don't make these mistakes, check it all out."

I told Jill about my talk with Jack and how funny and yet how serious it was. "Maybe you and I should think about what we really want from our honeymoon."

"You mean honestly?" asked Jill.

"It makes no sense if we're not honest," I said. "Just think about it."

There is a primal urge to expose your lover to the land you come from. It is as though you had met in Act II of a drama and you both needed to relive Act I to understand your stage characters. This is the root of our honeymoon experience.

Look at my country, look at me, I say. Look at Yorkshire, see me in the rugged cliffs, the churning ocean, the gentle dales, the vast moors. These are the lines for my character in this play, just as are, for you, the big skies, the blazing sun, the huge ocean and the yearning redwoods of California. See our differences: see our correspondences.

And there is a script, a geography to our families. This father is a mountain: that one a mound. This mother a canyon: that one a valley. This sister a stream: that one a torrent. This brother a flat plain: that brother a high desert. Here they are, and this is how I play with them and play off them, so you may grasp where we all posture in this drama of my life.

I thought about my personal "honeymoon agenda."

Be sure to uphold our first marriage priority—keeping our

spiritual well-being, using prayer and meditation, and taking in sober meetings whenever available.

Introduce my family to Jill.

Show Jill the places, the countryside, where I grew up and which helped mould me.

Expose Jill to some of the culture of England, the architecture, the museums, the art, the cuisine, the theatre.

Assess Jill's ability to cope with a foreign environment and travel. Flexibility, adaptability.

Stuart was really serious about this honeymoon agenda idea. He sat at his desk writing his list of five things. I was lying on the couch in front of the fireplace. "I thought you were going to write a list, too," he said, very executive.

"I'm done," I said, "and it's simple. One, doing you; two, you doing me; three, doing each other; four, other ways; five, starting over. That's all I really want, time in your arms. No phone."

"Aside from that," he said, "which goes without saying, I want you to really think about this."

"And if they don't match, the deal's off? I suppose this is one of your marketing tests." I was cranky because he was flying off the next day to see a client in Chicago.

Will he come back? With Laurie, I was the one who left—to go on the paperback book tour for *Bed/Time/Story* just after he was out of rehab. Left him with my kids, a house to run, and his job. He'd made it clear earlier, by retreating, that he had no gift for dealing with teenagers. At least he'd waited until I returned to disappear. I've always told the story my way, as one quick, sharp exit.

No plot point in any relationship between two smart people can be summed up in snappy lines, especially the ending. People's time in my life are moments of their real lives, not parts of my movie.

But I don't want to go on the honeymoon, not yet. I want to stay in Connecticut, talk with everyone who comes to the wedding, take cake and flowers to my parents in New York.

Later, we could go to London to pick up the Jaguar. I'll go see the statue of FDR for my father, and then we'll drive up to Yorkshire to meet Stuart's family. In fact, the trip will make sense. The marriage vows will make a subtle, but powerful difference in our relationship, all our relationships. We'll need a kind of blank territory to test out this new dynamic, to give it some perspective.

So, we'll go on a honeymoon. I'll try to throw off all my past references, try not to call home when I'm over there. Stuart's taking me by the hand into his world, his time, and I mustn't let my past take away the impact this experience will have on our future.

Twenty-Five

Falling in love is a lot about finding out who your friends are. Falling out of love is easier for them, easier to sympathize. All they have to deal with is the same old you. With falling in love, there's someone else, and changes in you as you shift around. Happiness isn't always a thrill when it's not your own, especially in exasperating people who will not keep it simple bliss.

It felt like simple bliss for us the morning we married, even with the phone ringing off the hook. "Do you wear a hat to church? Can our two friends here from L.A. come too? Do you mean noon sharp? Does Western mean jeans? Are you excited? Will there be room for kids? Is it a long drive?"

Martha arrived early with a cheerful team and miles of calico to drape the long picnic tables. All commanding charm, she supervised heaps of baskets and bowls rolling out of pickups as she brought Topanga to its liveliest extreme as a ranch framed by grand pines with goats, sheep, and ponies wandering around bales of hay in the open garage. Ivy and wildflowers loop along the porch rafters and fence rails.

My sister, Joy, was in charge the minute she woke up, buoyant with a kind of awesome rabbinical authority I hate when it's turned on me, but adore when she's using it on someone else. Today she was carefully keeping the borders where she sensed I wanted them.

Stuart had slept in his house last night with Philip and Susan amid the rest of the packing boxes.

I wound a wreath of tiny ivy leaves through my hair and watched Johanna in the mirror as she zipped my dress. Such curious feelings she must have, dressing her mother for one more wedding at a time when I should more rightly be helping her plan her own. As friends arrived, she played the amused buddy for the adolescent mom.

This day was bordered for me by the sense that I would not see my father again. But there was also the wonder of taking off for my first trip out of America, all the meaning I'd given that.

As Jeremy and Johanna drove me to the church in a Mustang convertible, the town was as bright as a set in an old MGM musical. Inside the church, sweet tones and bells ringing. The quality of serenity, the still light of the church seemed to link us all together. The seats were filled with New Yorkers, New England buddies, and L.A. friends, all in Western hats, fringed buckskin, and denim shirts. As I stood with Jeremy and Johanna in the doorway, faces from every decade of our lives, witnesses of every romance, triumph, and collapse turned their wide smiles on us. Friends from each of our separate and varied campaigns who have been here—advising, warning, encouraging, teasing, comforting, always coming back to us.

Ted Hoskins was the definitive minister, glowing in his robes. And there, with Susan and Philip at his side, was Stuart. The flower girls, Priscilla and Claire Gilman, started down the aisle first, then Johanna and Jeremy just ahead of me.

"Here Comes the Bride" started and I was eighteen, freer, gayer than I'd ever been. In my white cowboy boots I ran; holding up my skirt with one hand and the white bouquet with the other, ivy trailing behind me, I ran to Stuart. He stood there beaming in his denim frontier shirt with the blue satin stallions embroidered on the yoke, polo boots, and English riding breeches. Perfect. How fast could I get to him? Perfect. I flew past the laughing faces from hundreds of scenes of my life. Perfect. I stood next to Stuart now, clutching his hand as Ted held up his broad hands and beamed down across us with the richest blessing of love I had ever felt. And my heart was forever safe.

At the end of the ceremony we all joined hands for the Lord's Prayer. Then, to "Oh, What a Beautiful Morning," Stuart and I led our new family out of the church, past all these well-wishing faces, all the suspended cynicism, all this hope. After all, if *we* could do it . . .

Twenty-Six

~

It was the morning after our Midsummer's Day wedding and we were landing at London Heathrow. Exactly a year had passed since our first night together when I'd been shocked to find that Jill had never been out of the United States. "I just like cars and driving," she'd said, "and I don't need to leave America to do that."

"I think that a writer ought to travel," I'd said, "have adventures, see new places. If you ever went to England with me, I'd have a great car at the airport, a Jaguar, and drive you to your heart's delight through kinds of country you'll fall in love with." And here we were, getting into a splendid, wine-dark Jaguar, ready for the road.

But first, London. The Hyde Park Hotel set among the Knightsbridge crush of fashionable shops—Harvey Nichols, Harrods, and every name in fashion. I figured the shopping would make Jill more at home. Museums later. And of course, on the park side of the hotel, there was quintessential Englishness in the horse riders galloping along Rotten Row. We did all the things tourists do, because they're so interesting, and need not be discussed later since everyone's done them.

"Do you only have double beds?" I asked quietly. The main thing if you're American is to lower your voice. "And I'll need pillows that don't have feathers, please." I looked out the window of the Hyde Park Hotel. Stuart and the man showing us to our new room exchanged a patient look. "You ought to ask them to clear out the mini-bar," I whispered to Stuart.

"I will get to that"—he'd about had it— "after you've finished your requests."

"We always have a fight when we first go anywhere new until we make love," I reminded him, "and this is very new for me."

He called room service for tea, then said, "I'm going for a walk, do you want to come along?"

"No." I really wanted to sleep. He meditates when he walks.

I stood with my teacup, staring out over the bright green park reaching as far as I could see. The frail rain did not discourage the formal English riders in the park. England looked exactly like I dreamed it would. And from the minute you land, everyone sounded so wonderfully *English.* He must never imagine this is how I am thinking. How to do a sort of 'been around' cool?

I picked up the phone to call home, but the last thing I had done at the airport in New York was call my father to tell him he'd be in my heart every moment, but that I wasn't going to call. "Do you understand?" I'd asked him. "Yes," he said, "you don't want to find out I'm not here."

•   •   •

I fell in love with London very much the way I fell in love with Stuart. Right away.

"I don't walk," I warned him when our window shopping down Sloane Street extended beyond the stores. But we walked by rows of silent, private parks, where behind the dark hedges you'd see a nanny telling stories to two small children. "Trust me," Stuart said, as we moved into the creamy Georgian splendor of Eaton Square.

Each day he walked me into a piece of history or a literary scene I'd adored. The connections, the memories, images from books and films, were such a gift, I didn't notice the walking. He'd remind me of a beheading here, a Dickens scene there. I cased the people around me. You could be eccentric in London, where up-to-the-minute acceptability was beside the point.

After a few days in London, we went north on the motorway. "Isn't this a bit fast?" said Jill.

"Not really, Jill. The Jag comes alive at about ninety."

"I love it," she said, "faster."

Before going to my home in Pontefract, we drove to York for the evening and checked in at the Dean's Court Hotel. "I wanted you to be here, next to the glorious York Minster, to celebrate your first night in my country," I told Jill. "And it is said that if you make love here in the shadow of the Minster you will become an honorary Christian—sort of a baptism."

"You lie," she squealed, "but I'll try it anyhow, and maybe you'll become an honorary Jew."

"More like a horny pagan" was my retort, as I dove into bed.

My father and mother, sisters and brother, with their attendant mates and offspring, gathered to welcome us in the small living room of my mother's cottage. Only my oldest sister, Marjorie, was missing. She'd fled to Australia when I sailed for the U.S., and she rarely communicated, although after many years of silence, quite amazingly, I received a loving letter from her on my wedding day. My other prewar sister, Marlene, was here. One sister, Lynn, and my brother, Philip, are of a different era—postwar-soldier's-return children born after I'd left home.

The room was crowded with bodies and with ghosts. Only the food had substance. I could commune with the hams and meat pies, flirt with the puddings and chocolates, communicate with the cheeses. The people were less substantial. They flickered across like pages in a photo album, recognised like snapshots more than felt in the pulse and the blood.

The apartness was inevitable and understandable. With spare and boisterous flying visits, we had been physically apart for nigh on thirty years. Different lives in different places. And there would be mixed feelings, perhaps a touch of envy for the one who went away, became a "success," comes back with a "Hollywood" wife, driving a Jag. And why doesn't he come down to the pub and drink a few pints like he used to do?

So I stood there as in a dream, where my mouth is moving but no words come out. Struck dumb by the memories of the other side of success. Oh, how distance lends enchantment to the view! Enchants and distorts the grinding labour, the sacrifices, the failures, the pity of those who were trampled on, left behind. Will Jill understand any of this, see that I'm apart and that this will never be a family for her, the way she imagines family?

I sat and drew with the younger kids, partly to keep them quiet so Stuart would neither kill them nor want to leave too early. It meant so much to his mom to have him there. Stuart's father had nothing to say. He just sat there, smoking stubby cigarettes, like a battered old factory, smoking away.

Stuart's brother said, "Oh, things are okay, I guess, the way they are," because he couldn't change it anyway, could he? He saw only the sadness in everything, his dark eyes sizing up our faces, going round the room from one to the other, circling, circling, like a brooding cameraman finding the bleakest image, the take to confirm the mood in which he works his days.

Then someone suggested we should play the "wishes game," where everyone comes up with a secret wish. Stuart's mother looked at him with flirty challenge. "I've always dreamed of a Scarborough cottage for my last days, which I know I won't have, but it's what I wanted when I was a young girl before the war," she said. She had no idea how to begin to ask her oldest son who he was, where he'd been most of her life. She was sixteen when he was born.

Stuart never acts touched or affected by heartstrings, but I knew him enough to know that if he had the money, he'd get his mother a cottage like that. He loves giving—and he's so eager to give you what you want. His mom understood that, too—might even have been that way herself if she'd had the chance—but to her we had money. It's hard to understand someone else's idea of what they can and cannot afford.

Like most family events, this reunion felt staged; everyone on for a moment, then the long mystified silences until someone took a turn with yet another memory, usually to someone else's embarrassment.

I thought of our wedding day, how fast we'd left, and of what we'd left behind. I thought of our children, and doubted they'd sit across from one another like this, waiting to see who'd talk next. I imagined them, instead, scattering back to their own scenes, just as Stuart's nieces and nephews were itching to do, glancing at the door, waiting for the chance to leave.

Our wedding day had been full of conflict for my children. There had been no turning back. I had given them no chance, not a single moment when they might have said, 'don't go, don't leave us with this'. I had trained them to go on with the show, because dealing with the reality of my father's death was too hard. I couldn't face my father's death. I couldn't even face letting them know it might happen. Because, then, we'd all know. Then it would be real, not just another fear I couldn't face.

We all said we loved each other and good-bye, closed the photo albums, and piled into the Jag. Jill and I were heading for the ocean, to Scarborough, the magnificent scenery and the sleazy, fish and chip and bingo promenade, all as real as the food on my mother's table. The only ghosts there would be those we contrived for our own saga.

Jill took me to task when I revealed my feelings about my family to her on the drive to Scarborough. "That's not fair," she said, "they are warm and generous, and they clearly admire you. I was watching in the 'wishes game,' here we were, strangers really, and they were saying, 'how can we know each other.' Your nieces were so tentative about their wishes to hike across America."

"None of the wishes were real except my mother's," I said, "because she figures I can get that cottage for her."

"Well, you do send her money," Jill said. "Look how our lives must seem. We must look like we have a fortune. "

Yes, I was the one who left home and did very little to keep in touch. My checks to my mother were not much of a consolation for years and years of absence. And I was in my early days of sobriety—a couple of years and I was indulging in self-pity. Had I made appropriate amends to my parents and family? I had to think about that.

He was mine again. We were on the road. Heather, like California's chaparral, stretched out, the horizon bright ahead the way it gets when the sea's just beyond.

Was this what Stuart felt when we were alone again after a visit with my family? Was escape what he had in mind? Like love is a wild bird—and family a cage.

Oh, speed, yes. You can't go too fast on roads like these, like L.A. roads, all empty and wild in my dreams. I put my feet up on the dashboard, knees to my chest, my head back so I can see the sky through the roof window. Is loving him a lot about our driving? Take away fast cars, empty roads, and long wide highways and what do we have? But cars are sex—all chrome and hard, gleaming style; speedy, dreamy escapes, long, lost hours. Music catching the swerve and action, building up our appetite. Appetite, yes. Food. Where does chocolate end and sex begin? He is ice cream, red meat, and fresh, warm bread. I do long to eat him up.

"Would you pull over to the side of the road so I can tear you apart?"

"Sure," and he did and we went for each other, then drove on to Scarborough where we could finish with the sound of the waves crashing below.

"No," I said, when we were shown to our room, "it has to have a view of the sea." And when I got that, "I need a desk, here, or a table by this window. To write."

I'd found my heart's home, and I was not missing a minute of it. I felt it coming, like you know when you're having a big triumphant dream. I'd felt it coming as he sped across the moors, going off to the end of the world, a rhythm of land, dipping and swerving through centuries I'd never dreamed I'd see. I'm feeling them, seeing them now—all the land I'd read about in books by women who walked here, rode here, loved and lost and died, but not before they passed the spirit of all this onto their pages. It's half of him I fell in love with and half of this, his land. I want to wrap my arms around it and never leave.

Stuart was walking on the path winding round the base of the castle's cliff dashed by the North Sea. I sat at the shiny dark wood table they'd brought up, one shaky leg and a leather insert scratched by old pens, and I started writing.

Another woman once sat in this round tower room. She'd come to marry a northern prince on his way home from a Viking conquest. Ships took forever, but it had been six months. Patience was so different then. Maybe that was one reason they died so much younger; died of waiting to hear.

An hour went by and Stuart had disappeared beyond the great crouching cliff. I ran out onto the promenade, brushing aside a light veil of rain, and I saw him way up there, turning down now behind a jut. Now I'd found the trail he was on, and I was running up to catch him.

• • •

Later, as we turned onto the road down to London from Scarborough, I said, "Maybe everyone in love, every couple has its own 'road' story. Like kids have their continuing bedtime stories, always the same heroes. I have something in mind. Where were we when we were talking about minstrels?"

"We were in York," he said. "You were wondering about the sounds of minstrels strolling through the town, how it would have sounded centuries ago." He always remembers. "You were beginning a story. You said you'd come up from Westminster Abbey with a group of minstrels we'd met in York."

"Yes! It's a saga where we meet again in every century, and each time we meet we make the same mistake. But in this last century, we get it right."

"Oh, do we?" he said.

"Yes."

I looked over at him, "Is that too L.A.?"

"Probably." He was not crazy about this, but he will be.

"We want a karmic resolution, sort of happily ever after," I said.

"Of course we do," he said. "There are moments here and there, when we're looking at each other, making love, or just talking, when I'm seized by the conviction that we were destined for each other."

Twenty-Seven

The honeymoon was over and here we were, 35,000 feet over the Atlantic somewhere between London and New York, plugged into the Bee Gees on the headsets, twitching, grimacing, fingers snapping. This return trip seemed so much more pleasant, even the food tasted less like plastic. And, surely, our more relaxed state of mind colored everything rosy.

Over the intercom as we came in for the landing at Kennedy, an announcement: "There are messages in reception at the airport for the following people . . . Robinson-Shaw . . ."

"Something to do with the limo," I muttered. Jill was silent, and I thought she might be preparing herself for bad news.

The note on the message board was ominous: "Call Jeremy at the Scharys' Sutton Place."

I saw Jill on the telephone across from the luggage carousel, animated, her arms stabbing the air. She put the phone down and walked slowly over to me.

"My father died this morning. Jeremy's there and wants us to go straight over . . ." Then she was in my arms, not crying, not talking.

Words are devalued in the presence of death. This is, I suspect, a harking back to some other, deeper mode of expression, pre-verbal, before language and the chatter of relief mark, divide, and designate our grief and joys.

I wanted to be there when my father died; to hold him in my arms, to be sitting by his bed, my hands around his hands, pray-ing, silent with him, the way he was with his mother when the doctor held the mirror under my grandmother's nose and there was no breath. That was the way you showed the family someone was really dead, that it wasn't just a medical say-so. I wanted to be the one to close my father's eyes. My mother would find that too unbearable.

I clutched on to Stuart as we sped into the city, and thought of my father. All the years of fearing his death, the doctors dashing up the wide front stairs, pajama shirts hanging out under their jackets, the drives to the hospital. Such a powerful spirit in a fragile body.

I looked at Stuart, only a glance. Would he be relieved in a way? Would he now be the complete center of my attention? Did he know how often I had looked out at the North Sea and won-dered if my father's spirit was flying over on a last dash round to where his family came from in Russia? Did Stuart guess how often I'd sent a prayer to my father to have an easy day, to have no pain, to know I was there with him?

I thought of that last talk with my father, and Death, the word we never said when we sat beside each other in that hushed limousine. Did I know, as I think I did now, that it was to be our last talk? I thought of Jeremy. My father knew it would be hard on him, and now it was Jeremy's role to tell me. How bleak, how empty, and how desperate it will be at my parents' place.

Johanna was at the door when we arrived. She seemed stunned as the positions shifted and formed for the new roles. She was the most caring of my mother, who had taken on a protective coat of chemical isolation, but nothing would numb my mother sufficiently. My mother seemed to go mad months ago knowing my father was really going to die. It was what she'd feared most of all since they'd first met when she was nineteen, and now it was no easier than she thought it would be during all their years together when it had come so close.

My mother used to say to me, "You'll see," and "I hope you'll never see," wanting me to know what this kind of attachment was, wanting me to have it, but not have it. Now, as I saw her chalk-white in this chair, I started to reach for her to hold her, and she shook me away. "Don't try."

I remembered when my Grandfather Ted died. James Edward Cawthorne, a man who had been an occasional father to me. I held his dead body in my adolescent arms, touched his rosy face, as serene as it often was in the lively days, and the soft, silken shock of silver hair.

I left the house and followed the road, then the country lane, in the darkness. The first light of day's dawning and brown clodded earth in the fields, bird calls, and the sweet and rough smells of a Yorkshire country morning. There the images in my head found identity in the countryside. Symbols, natural noises, took the place of uttered sounds.

At Sutton Place the scene was the mixture as always: grief revealing itself, grief concealing itself, numbness and charade, the edge of hysteria, fringe of coma, the first drink in a drunk. So few of us have auditioned for this role. To the younger ones, there had been no other losses of this magnitude, so they were devoid of precedent. Their manners, movements and gestures were, for the most part, awkward or inappropriate. There was a difference in gender, maybe to do with female volubility versus male taciturnity, but this might be too simple an observation.

Jeremy's grief was sublimated in action, getting things done, being a responsible and capable performer for the father-grandfather, his stage manager still so close.

Miriam said she was numb, by which I inferred a conscious decision to quell all her feelings and deal with the etiquette of death and bereavement until the noise and the tumult ceased and she was left to mull on what widowhood meant in its complex mix of loneliness and narcissism, isolation and freedom.

After telling us Joy and her brood were on the way from Los Angeles, Jill's brother, Jeb, retreated to his father's old room, like a wounded animal to his lair. He was tight and curt, wanting, I felt, to be in charge and not be in charge, unable or unwilling to step out of character.

There were others, as there always are; for me faces without names, names without faces. Many of the faces seemed aged, as though grief had furred features like the insides of old kettles. Mourning makes us all more so; we become more of whatever our nature is. We exaggerate the roles assigned to us by nature and nurture, and our perceptions of others are magnified in the edge of the glass where distortion stays. We lose our centers of perception in the imbalance of a presence removed. Our senses must be reassessed and reordered. The hidden focuses need recalibration, new depths of field and feeling.

Jill did what she does so well. She comforted, she talked openly, she was solicitous of people's needs. She tried to have things her way, because she believed that this was more effective than a mishmash of styles and lack of style. She was holding her grief in her clenching hands.

Then a quietly reflective drive home to Connecticut, and I was holding on and praying for Jill.

We were tired and vulnerable, living on the periphery of reason with questions of inordinate triviality. 'Will we ever get to talk about our wedding?' There are frightened moments when we are naked like children and needy, and please hug and kiss us and tell us how good we have been. And the voice says, 'Now stop that nonsense. I really won't put up with it. You are one thousand years old, you have seen infinite births, copulations, and deaths. You are known for wisdom and courage (God knows where from!), so even if you don't feel like it, at least act like a grown-up.'

They used to say, "Grin and bear it." I understood that, and "muddling through," and all those wise things I later derided as simplistic. I was clinging now to those simple, wise things I no longer derided as simplistic. They are pre-Freudian saviors, infinitely more primitive and, therefore, more profound, and they were meant for persons of character, or those with a desire for character who look forward by dealing with today.

We slept a few hours and got up to enter the fray again. She left early, and I began the task of unpacking my worldly goods in a house inimical to my expansive nature. I should be working on the forthcoming assignment for Coca-Cola, but I couldn't address anything, even reading the mail, until I'd cleared a decent space for myself. I was thinking, coming out of the shower stall into a cramped bathroom and surveying the frightful mess of 'my office, my room,' that things had indeed come to a pretty pass. A serious period of adjustment looming; learning to share a house with Jill.

In late afternoon, I drove down to the Scharys. Joy was there now, we hugged closely. She looked distraught, many tears. "Her emotions are always so clear," Jill said.

The tone had changed. More circus. The release, I supposed, of an interregnum where it was clear there was no king so compelling, loving, and despotic as the king just dead. Indeed, no king or queen. So, perhaps we were witnessing a mild state of anarchy, a little akin to the behavior of conquering troops, not quite sure they could yet sack the city, but stoking up on food and drink and visions of spoils. It is in all of us, I suppose.

In my experience, there is nothing that clearly differentiates the aftermath of a death and the customs and behavior that surround it, from religion to religion, race to race, faith or no faith. It is the same pagan form and behavior tricked out in a cultivation of "specialness." The living room as stage, where caves or forest clearings once sufficed, is where the body had its temporal power, so clearly now gone save the books and pictures, relics of the life and power. Provision is made for feasting and for getting out one's feelings.

Beyond the funeral, there was to be an Anti-Defamation League memorial service. There was a great deal of sparring about who should speak, with Jill dissembling in courtesy to her brother and sister. She finally turned to me and asked what I thought she should do. "You should definitely speak," I said, "it's the right thing to do." God knew when she'd have time to write it, but I knew it would be more about her mother than her father.

The only thing I could do here of any use was attend to my mother, make it clear how much she gave him, how much so many women learned about loving from her—long ago, before any of these people here now will remember.

I couldn't separate my parents. I tried to own each one at different times in my life, but what I'd learned about marriage I'd learned particularly from my mother. Their happiest time was in Portofino when he was writing *Sunrise at Campobello.* She typed, he wrote, and they were as close as they'd always meant to be, as close and private as in the first years of their marriage when he was writing screenplays, and they were living in the Hollywood Hills.

Another late-night drive home and the air thick with feelings. Within me surges a tide of protective feelings, protecting Jill even more totally now that her father has gone. Right now this primal feeling was so powerful I could almost sense the touch of the sword in my hand, feel the weight of the shield on my arm, the sinister struggle to protect the woman, the mother, the guarantor of the future, our survival. These feelings are as deep inside as the sexual drive, and perhaps they are simply strands of the same cloth. At the same time that I knew I would die for my lover, I knew I must make love to her.

I woke up wanting Jill, and I took her in the early light, clearing the corridors of my overstuffed brain.

Twenty-Eight

~

The consulting business was now my life and I could pay the rent. A divestiture in Pennsylvania, a strategic review in Wisconsin. Travel all over the country, often away from Jill.

The irony of my situation was inescapable. The age-old conflict between desire and need and submerging one or the other is never successful.

The breadwinner propaganda never ceases: be a good sport; behave like a gentleman; pull up your socks and put your shoulder to the wheel; and above all, be a good provider. All euphemisms for 'get out there and kill the animal—you have to eat, don't you?' So we coerce ourselves with numbing tasks for paychecks and titles, leave the pen and the paper, the brush and the piano, sedate ourselves with "success" and "power."

There were a couple of ways I was trying to make life palatable. On the creative front, I'd made some space to write, to talk to writers, to talk about writing. Sometimes this was encouraging, like the talk and reading at the Southport Literary Society where

I had a warm reception to my readings. And on the business front, whenever there was a long trip, I tried to take Jill with me.

On a business trip to Phoenix, I had a chance to detour via Albuquerque and visit my oldest child, Stuart Jr., and to introduce my new wife, since he missed the wedding for reasons I still didn't understand. There he was at the airport gate, smiling, trimmed beard and hair—the hippie assuming responsibility, looking very smart. I was touched he'd made an effort; the off-white bush jacket I'd sent him, blue jeans, etched cowboy boots. After hugs and bristly kisses, his rap began—"speed rap," I called it. It flowed on its wondrous, whirling eddying rush until we left Albuquerque. Loving, warm, and so at ease with me and with Jill.

He was intuitive and perceptive and had a plan. He drove downtown, straight to his workplace, the ambulance service, where he introduced us to his fellow paramedics. And then in the back of a brand-new ambulance, "This is my office," and he rattled off a rundown of all the equipment, the medication, the uses for all the gear.

Then, confusingly, he had pressure pads stuck to my chest and I was hooked up to a heart monitor. He ran the scan, pulled out the graph, and handed me the strip with a full technical explanation. But that wasn't what I heard or felt. What I was really feeling was my son touching my heart. What I really experienced was the sad, yet joyful, love of four long years of separation suddenly erased, the bitter regret for what was lost dissipated in these priceless, heartfelt moments.

"Your business heart is just fine, Dad," said Stuart, "but . . ." a long pause, "what about your poet's heart?"

"I have to make a living, you know, son," I said.

"I guess so," he said, "but you don't want to wake up one day and find you've won a bank account and lost your soul."

"You're dead right, Stu," I said, "and I try to keep a balance with my higher power, prayer, and meditation."

"It needs more than that, Dad. You've been working since you were a kid. Now you need to express yourself, share your knowledge, pull all that wisdom together. That's why I believe you started drinking. You had something to say, but it was all drowned in soaps and detergents and the money stuff. Now you're not on the booze, you have a chance to get it right this time."

"I'll try," I said. "I love you."

He dropped us off at our motel to leave our bags and then whisked us away to Sandia Peak, to the tramway up to the restaurant. Stuart Jr.'s dinner talk was heady. Reincarnation and karma sent him dizzying through Hindu, Buddhist, Zen teachings, his own experiences in communes and with mystics, his own readings, understandings, perceptions, insights. Jill and I simply sat there and marveled at this outpouring.

"I was deeply touched by the whole affair, obviously," I said to Jill back in the motel. "First he tells me he loves me, in fact demonstrates it in his ambulance. And second, I feel that the outpouring of knowledge was a way of saying to me, 'look Dad, I may have been a college dropout, but I've learned a great deal along my alternative pathway.'"

"He's amazing," said Jill, "and I really do understand. The whole sixties scenario, but an activist, not just talk—although he's certainly a great talker."

Beyond all this, I sensed a penetrating pathos in my son's life. He was estranged from an uptight society. I felt a kinship with that outsiderness, with his deep and different values in a world of old symbols and rituals. But my sadness was suffused with the warmth of our visit, the rekindled love and memories of those seven years when he was my only child; that little boy I took on walks, with whom I flew paper airplanes and fired off rockets in the park, and who always said on the way home, "Tell me a story about you and the airplanes." Now he was telling stories to his father.

Pleasantly, I found that the business needs could be dealt with expeditiously; a few hours in Phoenix, a half day in Tucson, and all this could be interspersed with sightseeing and adventure, which was good writing material for us. Life is a rough draft.

The next day, business attended to, we drove north to Paolo Soleri's visionary city of Arcosanti. We explored Arcosanti and its metal workshops, those marvelous bells, coruscating bells, jingling merrily in every imaginable tune and chord. We followed a trail down into the canyon, past the cacti, across the dry streambed, climbing up to the final escarpment, when we turned to look across sweeping, seemingly barren ranges, grassy tablelands, and forested eruptions.

I never thought I'd see Arcosanti. I'd had a Soleri bell by my door forever but my family had never been big travelers. Maybe that was part of what drew me to Stuart—the energy of the opposite. He wasn't impressed by Arcosanti. "A tourist attraction created by hippies, an inferior Disney World in a place where it isn't needed," he said.

The point was he'd gotten me here. "You'll get me round the world, I guess," I told him later, as we looked out over the mountains around Sedona, "if we get a chance."

"No," he said, "if we *make* the chance, if we *take* the chance."

~~~~~

Farther north in Sedona the majesty of the mountains was unsullied. In the nearby pueblos there was integrity after the contrivance of Arcosanti. Here man had delved an urban complex into a mountainside, becoming a part of the terrain, overwhelmingly simple.

On the ride back to Phoenix, Jill said, "Maybe that's what we saw in each other, in different ways. Both of us take chances, and when they don't work, because we're the way we are, we won't blame each other."

"At the risk of sounding pedantic," I said, "I'd say that I see in our travels today a great metaphor for love and marriage, or maybe more than one metaphor. I sensed a huge lesson in humanity; how some visionary projects can be just that—just visionary, not practical or workable. While the little things—say, the Arcosanti bells—can provide so much pleasure and satisfaction."

"Are we trying to do something impractical?" asked Jill.

"I don't think so. We're trying to live together in harmony, and perhaps tougher, we're trying to write and to make a living."

"What else?"

"I'm still sorting out my feelings about this trip," I said, "but I'm warming to the idea that we can be together through all kinds of situations and keep learning new things together. The more new things we experience together, the richer will be the memories we can look back on. Just consider what memories those mountains around Sedona must have."

"Well, I'm convinced of one thing," said Jill, "and please don't take this the wrong way. You're more of an artist than a businessman."

• • •

The months rolled by. "I never see you," I heard Jill say more and more.

"I miss you, too," I heard myself say, "and I never see my writing desk except for business reports."

The balance was shifting. The plaudits and paychecks I got from clients weren't offset sufficiently by the drudgery of the logistics. Drives to airports, flights, car rentals, drives to hotels, meetings, flights, drive home. All solo. Gunslinger.

As the nights grew longer and the weather harsher, Jill was more and more worried by my travels, blizzards in Wisconsin, plane delays, the separation.

"We should do something different," Jill said, after picking me up at La Guardia in a blinding snowstorm. "We can't keep doing this, it's wearing you out. I'm missing you terribly, and you're only writing those endless reports. I know the money's good, but this isn't why we fell in love and married." She was absolutely right, of course, but how would we change things? "Maybe we should relocate where the weather's better," she added.

"Relocating is a hell of a trauma," I said.

"Let's talk it over with Ted Hoskins later this week," said Jill.

"If we make it home tonight through this storm."

"That's why we have the Jeep," said Jill.

Twenty-Nine

I was waiting for the plumber when my mother's nurse called. My mother had thrown all my father's hats out the window, pulled his award plaques off the walls, and she was about to pitch out all his papers.

"Put my mother on the phone," I said. Of course. Today was their wedding anniversary.

I heard her gasping hysterically, devastated, "I want to die. You don't know what it's like to lose someone you love." Even in the midst of grief, love must be unique.

I sped down to the city, walked into her apartment, and burst into tears. She was wild with despair, her face like Munch's *The Scream*. I held her close but carefully, she was so frail. One arm had already been broken and badly mended, and her heart was pounding like a small bird, pounding as if it would come out of her chest.

Could I listen to her the way she would have listened to me? The way she used to listen to her models, like a fine confessor, sweeping with the brushes, stroking the canvas. I could say anything to my mother when she was lost in the trance of the character she needed me to be—the way she'd lose herself in all the characters of all the friends, the actors, the racy young models she'd hire to pose. They'd come around to my mother's studio through the garden gate, around past the gardener's shed down by the tennis court. They could tell her their hardest stories, which she'd then tell me to get me used to the idea life wasn't all so easy. My mother told me from the beginning that I must be my own person, hold on to my dreams. Hard to hold tight to my dreams when I felt the resentment of a man lowering his dreams to support me so I could keep mine going.

My mother's bravest moment had been giving up the house, her painting studio, her staff, and selling so many things while my father was working on his next play. She packed it all up and went East. While she was packing, I gave her the first bud on a twig from the peach tree in our backyard, and she'd sent it to my father in a letter.

Where was my mother going now? Had she decided to die?

A friend talked to me about a man she cared for who was told he had cancer. His doctor felt the tumor. The man went out to Santa Fe to work with an Indian medicine man and returned home, the tumor gone. It was simple, the medicine man had explained, "You had not decided to die." He knew his family needed him and he decided he had more to give. I think my father decided to die when his last play failed, when he realized he wouldn't be able to support his wife, as his father had failed to support his mother. Love didn't pay the rent.

Suddenly, my mother was very sharp with me. "You have to get rid of things in life. You need to change. You would never really have made your own life as long as our house on Marlboro

Street was there. Remember that. Your kids won't ever really move out as long as you have their house."

"How can I trust what you say when you're so crazy one minute and smart the next? Stuart hates my house."

"Of course he does, it's not his house. Men are that way."

I wondered, seeing my mother this broken after almost half a century of loving one man, if it wasn't easier never to love like this—never to take the risk of such a great loss.

She had pulled out her manila envelopes of letters and sketches; her journals and diaries; and her letters to my father during all the times he had to travel without her. And travel was harder then, especially since my parents wouldn't fly until their last years.

My mother handed me one of her letters from January 1959. It had a note in it I'd written to her, along with a sketch of Jeremy she'd done when he was eight months old:

> *Dearest Dore Darling . . . it isn't ever that people find fresh new years and constant love and excitement that seem to bless our lives. We have the treasure that "isn't ever" and, therefore, as rare as possible. I'm sending the sketch as a keepsake . . . the time will pass quickly . . . I'll be thinking of you and the play all the time. More than that, I love you—hold this dear—please take care of yourself,*

and the letter swirls and spins in circles of loving phrases.

"You can have all of it," my mother said, "but don't waste your time. Life goes very fast. At least you're in love."

"You taught me how to do that," I said.

Tonight, cunningly disguising my writer and poet identity by appearing as the husband of Jill Robinson, I attended the Poets & Writers Tenth Birthday Party at Roseland with Jill.

Jill had been wretched all day long for any number of no-good reasons; no-new-clothes angst, the not-finishing-her-book angst. Whereas my day had been riotously happy, starting out with the Wagoneer bursting into flames as I went through Fairfield to pick up our housekeeper. Very efficient fire brigade in Fairfield.

That evening up the stairs at Roseland, and Jill was in her seventh heaven; the paparazzi, camera-clicking, flash-popping us to frames of astral celebrity. It could be addictive, heavily habit forming.

Barbara Goldsmith and Lynn Nesbit had a table for a bunch of us that included Ann Beattie and Donald Barthelme. Then coming off the dance floor, joy exploded over Jill. Lauren Bacall, surging through to Jill for hugs, kisses, well wishes, and dishing dirt. Great lady. Back on the dance floor and an on-the-floor interview with us by *People* magazine. Neat.

I danced with everybody all night long, before we split at midnight for a diet-busting deli repast. Jill should be in a better frame of mind for a little while.

We had a stupid row after we got home last night and I woke up still with a free-floating resentment. I made a decision; I was not going to the morning meeting. It was not right for me today, nor was it right for such an appearance to be construed as something other than it was. The separation from Jill, my animal brain told me, must be directly connected with the bad scene last night.

She came into the bedroom, dressed and ready to go. "I'm not going to the meeting," I said, "I want to rest." She pleaded, tried beating on me, and then, resisted, she knelt down, grabbing on to me, and sobbed. "I am not going," I said again. She left, returning to pound on me again. "Tell me," I said, "did Laurie disappear after scenes like last night? Did you drive him away?" I think she answered, "Not at first, but then sometimes." I knew now why Laurie disappeared on occasions and, perhaps, ultimately walked out of Jill's life.

There was a brief encounter late in the afternoon and a profusion of apologies, flood of remorse. "A slip," Jill said, "I might as well have been on speed." I still felt some distance. Was it suspicion, rather than resentment, that troubled me, or the natural wariness of a clawed animal after a fight? She went out early, so I had the night to myself for catching up.

You see, it was all well and good to talk about making money to buy time for writing, but maybe it couldn't work out that way. There must be a way, and part of it had to come from some resolution of how much energy I could give to supporting Jill in her struggle with her work. Business, marriage, support, and writing was a pretty tall order, no matter how much reciprocal support one got from one's mate. It took time to unfurl, tease the fringes, draw a thread, loop the loops again.

A sort of half-life. Some of me with those trained urges to compete—shouldn't I be soliciting business? And some of me wanting to muse, dawdle, wander, and receive the revelation; perceive the revelation when it appears. Yet again, another part of me perhaps could not recognize pondering from procrastinating. Without help it was too much for us.

"He talks about *Matthew Six:24*—'no man can serve two masters.'" I smiled at Stuart, all fake generosity. I hated Ted Hoskins to see that I wasn't the loving Christian partner, but I'm not. "That's his book about the man who can't be the spy and the writer at the same time, about how he can't write political analysis and his novel. But he expects me to be the Executive Wife *and* the Writer."

"The wolf is always out there," Ted reminded us. "Even during the big years when it doesn't seem to be out there, you have to stand by your mate to protect against the wolf."

"Yes," Stuart said, and looked at me. "The wolf was there when we met, when you were writing and rewriting. It will be there when the reviews come out, when people buy or don't buy the book. Of course the wolf is always there, Ted, and I suppose we have to feed it all the time."

"We can take turns," I said.

Ted encouraged us to start talking about a new path. The worst thing when you're both scared is to decide not to talk because you'd worry each other. The idea is not to nag each other or to panic each other, but to place the broken construction on the table between you, make a list of what needs fixing and what you each might be willing to do.

"Or what we're each capable of," I said to Stuart. " I know what is broken—the house. And I don't believe we can fix it to any degree you'll like."

"And we'll need money." He smiled, as close as he sometimes came to a smile.

There must be new resources I could tap. Where was the help for me? I supposed Ted indirectly helped me by helping Jill. Thank God that I am by nature positive and optimistic. And yet, sometimes I felt that things weren't working out right for me as a writer. It was costing me much more per month to live than it did as a bachelor, which is not to say I preferred bacherlorhood. I loved Jill and much of my life with her, but when the clouds gathered over Jill, the gloom of dissatisfaction, the rankness of soured expectations, the effort of providing becomes burdensome, the energy which should thrust forward was dragged backward.

Today, I called a real estate broker to put my house on the market.

I understood, and think back over those long, lonely nights when I had everything exactly my way, saw who I wanted when I wanted, hung around, bending their ears. It was my turn to be the listener, the lover. When you love the man, feminism means taking your turn at the plow. Talk the talk, walk the walk.

A good way to find love is to make a change in where you are. And then a good gift for your marriage is a change if you can see you need it before it's too late. Often something comes along and kicks off this change: someone is fired or the work just stops. You *have* to change.

"Maybe the most important thing we do as parents," I said to Stuart, "is show our kids we can change, that nothing is impossible to face." I was thinking about my house, but also about my mother, who I always thought would die right after my father died.

"I'm moving back to California," my mother told us, shortly after we arrived at her apartment. "Joy called last night. She has talked to people, and I'm going to live at the Motion Picture Relief Home."

I was shocked. "You can't, not with all those old people."

"Jill, what do you think I am?" my mother said. "I'm just as old, and at least I won't be alone. I think it's a good idea. Joy will always be around, and it's only a long-distance call."

Miriam was a miracle. From that scared sliver of a woman to this lively, wiry bird fluttering her wings, rolling her eyes, and dying to be applauded for the hairdo, the apartment décor, the life in her. What a turnaround for her, and what a blessing for Jill.

"I could even phone you, like a real mother, when I'm driving him crazy!" Jill was hugging and hugging her mother, as though reunited through space and the ages.

There was an offer on Jill's house and everything flew into panic stations. The tension was high voltage.

The next day was damn close to being the breaking point. I saw smoke curling up through the heating grills. Was the house going to burn down? Did I care? I steeled myself, went down, and opened the basement door. Steam pushed out everywhere! I wanted to switch something off, but I was too scared to go farther inside. The water heater had blown up!

Not 'Pray to God and row to shore,' but 'Pray to God and row, just row.' I sensed that we were now rowing away from Jill's house, from Connecticut, perhaps even from America.

Stuart's favorite line is, 'It will be revealed.'

"So," I snapped, "I'm selling my house, we don't know where we're going to live. Nothing has been revealed."

"It will," he said.

We were packing some things up, putting other things out for the tag sale. I was considering smashing him on the head with the frying pan, when the phone rang. It was a writer I knew, Barbara Howell. She and her husband were in New York, could we come in and have dinner with them?

Stuart was cross. He had a project to finish next week. "I don't want to hear other writers talk about their work when I haven't got a minute to even look at my book."

"I don't think her husband is a writer," I said. "I think he's in business."

"Oh, sure," he said, and we drove to the city in stony silence.

Alan Woltz, Barbara's husband, had just become the head of a large international company and was moving to London. Alan was familiar with Stuart's career at Procter & Gamble and asked Stuart if he'd consider coming to London for a year or so to help sort out the huge conglomerate he managed. Everything moved amazingly fast, and they hammered out a deal over coffee after our dinner together.

"It has been revealed," Stuart said on the way home, "we should go to London."

"But will you have time to write?" I asked.

"Of course," he said. "I've agreed with Alan to take one day a week off, and then I'll add one day every weekend. We'll have to see how that plays, but I can't miss out on this great opportunity."

"It's really a great gamble, isn't it?" mused Jill. We were having a snack and coffee at the Sherwood Diner a couple days later. "This

is where our affair started, and now we're married, and we're going to take this great gamble."

"I've been reading Joseph Campbell," I said, "and he would ask, 'Is it going to be the Quest for the Grail or the Wasteland? Are we going on the creative soul's quest or are you going to pursue the life that only promises security? Are you going to live the heroic myth or let circumstances manage you?'"

"We'll go for the Grail," said Jill.

Thirty

~

Jill, soft and warm morning curves, clambered on top of me. The hammering sounds must be the roofers. Jill felt sensuous, loving, but it was more like bears romping than a serious sexual encounter. I held her tight, squeezing her against my chest, so preoccupied with work that my head kept turning the sex off. Perhaps if it weren't for the roofers, Jill and I could really get into this. Now some bastard was knocking on the studio door. The tag sale people already? I put my robe on, opened the door, and stalked out as grouchy as can be.

"The sale isn't until tomorrow," I said to a couple of early birds, catching myself sounding like my old headmaster. "Tomorrow, Saturday. Someone will be here then to take care of you. I have nothing to do with this, nothing at all."

I simply had to find a time to be alone with Jill. The unformulated lovemaking hung fuzzy in my head. Too often, I still had the silly idea that sex needed a setting, a scenario, a time and place of infinite serenity. Silly, because sometimes when we'd been fighting very hard and had traveled beyond that point where words connect, the act itself always worked.

The tag sale should bring in at least $1,000. It should go for rent, but could buy a wonderful creation for Jill. It would be so outrageous, and I hadn't done that since the fantastic brown suede Kamali we picked out in New York. Just stopped in, tried it, and hoped the American Express card would go through. It's her best thing, she said.

Perhaps this was what the tag sale was all about: selling off flawed memories, dumping inappropriate fantasies, clearing out the debris of other occasions. It was not so simple as Jill having slept in that four-poster bed with so-and-so, or I used to do things with so-and-so on that Oriental rug. Although there might have been some of that with us, I felt it had more to do with different ways of experiencing life at other times.

The tag sale day arrived and was every bit as horrendous as we thought it would be. I couldn't deal with it. It frightened me. I had promised myself that I wouldn't ask what anything sold for, and I tried to hold on to this sanity, guiltily protecting myself on some treasured lithographs by setting a $50 price on each.

Johanna had left after helping out for most of the day. Some of the pieces sold must have held memories for her, like the whimsical rag doll she rescued from the sale. Before Jill and I met, Johanna was like a sister or mother to Jill. She is trying to 'show willing' and I respect that. Johanna has been sick so long that it's a delight to see her looking healthy, full of energy and humour. She will begin her first real job this week, and perhaps her life will start to come together.

It seems that I've been giving Jill hugs and kisses every few minutes during the long day, as much for my benefit as hers. She hated the people nosing and poking around the stuff outside. She might not have felt as secure anyhow, because it had been days, two or three, since we made love, which always centres both of us. Tonight perhaps, I thought, watching the log flames silhouette her body's curves.

The telephone rang, collect call from young Stu in Albuquerque. I felt an engulfing wave of pity for him, seeing him there alone, a small, unfurnished room, no family within a thousand miles. He was the only one of my three children born in a foreign country, the child we brought with us when we came to this golden land. Homeless again, it struck me. I pictured Stu Jr. at three years old, standing by me, holding my hand as the R.A.F. truck pulled our trailer away, watching the only home he'd ever known just towed away. His bedroom towed away, all of his years towed away.

The tag sale was finished, even though some man had still to come around tomorrow to bid on the remainders. We'd finished almost $2,000 ahead, but the money had already merged into some vagueness. Without even mentioning it, all of us sensed the passing of the old order, the end of this story, the new adventure beginning and the upcoming move to England.

Jeremy was driving me down to the city. He'd started work at a talent agency, staying during the week at a little apartment in New York. One afternoon last week, I'd gone to his apartment to take some books and things he could use. His place looked spare and temporary, as places do when you're on your way into your own life. I remember my mother being devastated by the sight of my first apartment, most of all the sight of me cooking. At first I thought this was because she was elitist, but as I grew up, I realized she'd wanted me to be an artist, a writer. She didn't know most of us spend a lot of our time in kitchens, too.

Today, I saw strong confidence in my son's face, but there was also a kind of defiance. It was a lot of work, inventing your own security. How did he see it? His mother had finally owned a home, a place that felt secure without rent collectors at the door, and now she was selling it all and leaving.

"How's your work going?" I asked him. "Is the agency interesting?" I tried to talk crisp, say what I meant fast.

"Mom, your father ran a studio, so you know as much as I do about how interesting it is," he said. "I try to make it interesting and some days it is, other days it's not."

Would I ever be able to ask him an interesting question? Do the interesting questions have uncomfortable answers? "Are you angry that I'm leaving?"

"You probably feel you've got a reason to go to London," he said, "and it's your decision. It's hard for Johanna, living in Norwalk, working for that vet."

"She's taking pictures for the paper," I said, "and has lots of friends. I'm going to London because Stuart has a job there. We all have our own lives."

"Then don't ask me how I feel about it," he said.

"Maybe we all need some space," I said.

"Maybe." He shrugged his shoulders, and I touched his arm lightly.

I'd talked a lot about the pull between love and work, but the pull between love and children was tougher, darker. My mother said it would be even if the love in my life was their own father. Maybe so, but I wouldn't have the guilt, and I knew putting Stuart first in my life cut deep.

• • •

Johanna came over to pick up the last boxes I'd set aside for her; mugs, our red kettle, the stone rabbit. Then she and I drove down to the city to visit my mother. It was the day before Stuart and I were to leave for England.

Johanna was quiet. We'd talked as much as she was going to about a relationship she was in, a guy she'd decided to live with. "You have to let me make my own choices," she said, "and mistakes, and maybe not make it so clear when you think it's a mistake. If that's possible."

There were tears quickening up in our eyes, and not just about today. It was about being apart, about the house, about me being so far away—about everything. We won't fix this, we won't get over this time any more than we've gotten over leaving L.A., losing her dad's presence, Laurie leaving us, getting over Johanna's first sweet boyfriend. You just build up emotional muscle and it makes you stronger, tougher. I didn't need to tell Johanna this today. She was learning it the hard way—by living it.

I watched the Connecticut and New York world going by. The bright sun made Manhattan glow like it does on a crisp morning when it wants you to feel there is no other place you want to live. We'd made a choice. My children were beginning to make their own choices, to have their own triumphs.

My mother was kneeling on the floor of her bedroom, papers all around her, tufts and swatches of old silk flowers spilling out of hatboxes with cabbage rose prints, russet manila folders plump with old letters.

"Does she realize I'm moving to England?" I asked her nurse, who just shrugged her shoulders in silence.

I knelt beside my mother, my arm around her shoulder, her

bones frail as porcelain. "Mommy, come, let's be together. Johanna's here. You know, I am going to London. Tomorrow."

"Jill"—my mother looked at me sharply—"of course I know. What do you think I'm doing?" She handed me an old letter on paper with the Marlboro Street address of the house I grew up in. "Read this," she said.

> *Dearest Dore, my darling love,*   *31st January 1959*
>
> *It was thrilling to hear about the reviews in Boston and I'm so happy for you and everyone and even for me. I love hearing about everything, but I miss you and when you read this, follow it with a wailing sound in the wilderness and that is me, right now, packing up everything.*
>
> *. . . Jill picked this little twig from the peach tree, which is in a hurry to blossom again, and I'm enclosing it for you, but there are peach blossoms on trees all over the world . . .*
>
> *So, yesterday I truly locked up the house. I finished tagging everything at 3:30 in the afternoon: Ship, Children, Sell, Appraise. I feel like a bride about to embark upon a honeymoon for the rest of our lives.*

"You see," my mother said, pulling the dried bit of twig from the envelope and handing it to me, "I know how you feel, but I want you to keep in mind that it's not so much an ending, but a bright romantic beginning."

Thirty-One

~

So it was that we said *au revoir* to Connecticut, New York, family and friends, and took up residence in London with typewriters. We were reinventing ourselves. Not without pangs of regret and shards of fear, but over and above these negative thoughts was the stimulation of adventure, new pages in our love affair, new experiences to share as the dyad, Jill and Stuart. On a dream and a prayer was how we did it.

At first it had seemed to be a crazy idea. "Not so crazy," "terrific idea, a change of pace," "nothing ventured, nothing gained," and on and on, with virtual unanimity among our friends.

"We'll have enough money," I assured Jill, "so we'll see what happens."

"Andrea Tana will help us find a place to stay," said Jill, "I'll call her right away." And a week later she'd found a two-floor flat for us in London.

"It's perfect," she'd laughed, "the address is Wimpole Street. Could that be more romantic?"

"Sounds like the movie *The Barretts of Wimpole Street.*"

"Exactly," Andrea said.

We hung my mother's painting in the dining room, our bell from Arcosanti by the stairs. My curved table sat right in our bedroom window, looking out at a tree as big and high as the old oak tree I looked out on when I was in Connecticut. But in London, around the tree, are the back windows, the courtyards, and brick walls of a world of Victorian and Edwardian houses, the offstage voices in the courtyard and the presence of love all around me. The sky rolls its weather by, changing lighting and climate with every hour, variations on the theme of gray.

I learned from London's dreamy pace that you could stay inside just to read. It would never occur to anyone that this was unreasonable. I met artists and writers who never went out, or we'd sit around each other's kitchen tables from Kensington to Primrose Hill. Then there was London's fast lane, an eccentric world of fancy, careless adventure. 'Come to our house in Gloucestershire this weekend, I've planted a medieval maze.' 'Oh, you're going to Eze Village, come see us at our place in Monte Carlo.'

There were Stuart's quick business trips. We'd been planning a weekend in Cornwall when he had to go to Berlin. He'd been back two days when Leo Lerman called from New York, asking if I'd care to go to Venice for *Vogue*, on the Orient Express.

"Stuart will never go," I said, "he's working hard."

"It's perfect for you two," Leo said.

"He won't go," I said.

"Tell him," Leo said.

"It will be perfect for us," Stuart said. "The Orient Express, think Agatha Christie, think *Death in Venice,* the Lido, the gondolas, the architecture. And I could use a break from the business stuff and a chance to think about writing, perhaps even write in a new place."

"I told Leo you'd love the idea," I said.

The Venice-Simplon Orient Express departed from Waterloo Station. Each coach was one-of-a-kind, and Jill and I were in a splendid one with marquetry and a frieze of roses and ovals featuring Rubenesque ladies. The actual train, Broadlands, "is the one that took Churchill off to his burial ground," a guard advised me.

After the countryside, the English Channel, with gulls hovering over our wake and the scrawny-jawed Folkestone cliffs, then the sterner, tanned Boulogne cliffs. The orchestra breaks into a Parisian medley to celebrate the coast of France.

We were high on the air and the rocking of the train on its silver wheels. My husband's arms and rose-colored sunlight on the mountains. The Sanchez negligee with the feathers feels at home here. I fling it off and slither closer to Stuart on the damask sheets. The breakfast tray arrived as dawn came over the Alps, with delicious brioches and croissants picked up, freshly baked, from a quick stop at Lausanne. And all the varieties of jam one could conceivably lick off each other's fingertips.

Now, from the crisp Alps, we plunged into the Simplon Tunnel out into golden light. It's green, terracotta, gold, turquoise, and it is Italy. "This really is!" All of Europe looks just like I'd hoped it would and feared it might not.

The manager of the Gritti Palace Hotel welcomed us to Venice and showed us to a room, yes, yes, overlooking a grand canal busy with boats and gondolas. There was music everywhere, in all the stones of the city. Was that Gabrieli I heard? We wandered into the church, a scattering of people among the wooden pews, a group of student musicians. It was the Conservatoire de Bienne and it was a rehearsal for "Concerto di Musica Rinascimentale." The glorious sounds seemed absolutely to fit the city of Titian and Old Masters.

Yet another rehearsal in the Church of San Stefano, *The Messiah.* There is something incongruous about any rehearsal of Handel's *Messiah,* when one wants to believe that each performance is divinely inspired, that saintly singers assemble and the score is revealed to them at the instant the conductor raises his baton to high heaven. As it is, a puny guy sitting next to me sidled up to the foot of the stage and sang a beautiful tenor solo, as if he had just passed by, liked the sounds and simply wanted to join in.

The most dramatic scenes in this city of drama were those with gondolas. At night after dinner on the veranda, here comes a squadron of gondolas, six abreast, lanterns flickering in romantic ecstasy at the basic baritone, the familiar songs, the indispensable accordion. There could not be horse-drawn cabs, six abreast, in Central Park, with music, nor gondolas anywhere else in the world. Gondolas are the drama, the logo as it were, of Venice, but more than anything else, I love the city's colors. They are my age as I see my age; warm, crumbling here, a pallor of decadence there, but sturdy as the earth tones and stones, mellowed and the soft menace of maturity.

Over coffee and biscotte at the Cafe Florian in the great plaza, I scrawl a love note to the city:

My Dearest Venezia,

It was love at first sight. That furtive love of adolescence, on street corners, in shop doorways, underneath the arches, walking, drifting, watching and waiting for the moment, the often unfulfilled moment, sensing the very essence of alone and palely loitering.

Yes, it was that stealthy love of early adventures among the shades, the whispers and cabals. Jinking in and out of the shadows of one's own fears and yet daring the darkness for the erotic oblivion of its romantic embrace.

I love you, Venezia. I want to be with you always in my heart at this café table, writing love songs and sagas across the ages with you and with my soul mate, Jill.

Love,
Stuart

I watched Stuart here, glowing, gentling down. This is what I saw in him that first night and for moments on our honeymoon. How fast he changes when there are memos to write, budgets to study, conferences to attend. It's as if I'd snapped down the shade in front of the man watching us: this gentle, brooding, reflective character disappears; the polished, cosmopolitan executive presides over our lives. Am I up to that pace? You might not know London had such efficiency as he commands.

Here, in Venice, Stuart is the writer, and I don't want to leave him. Does he know I see this difference? All the worlds I was sure I'd never see were opening around me. When you don't think you'll have the chance, you work out a rationalization that it doesn't matter, but now the more I see, the more it does matter. Stuart was there explaining, introducing me, backing everything I saw with history and legend.

But the executive returned. A few months after we returned to London from Venice, we had a big fight. I saw him as a dismissive authority and wondered, did he know me anymore? Like most people, the fights we have are triggered by the same things—usually over the infuriating techniques we each use to deal with fear. I'd guess most fights are about fear. Stuart had a lot of pressure; a job and the desire to succeed, his determination to write, and my homesickness. It's one thing to have the great idea, another to be living it.

London wasn't simply a romantic story where I could idyll into legends to see what I'd like as my history, prowling through dark mews and by creamy palaces. You don't know London until it decides to let you in, even though you may affect the easy shrug. You will always be the outsider. And it didn't help that one of my friends whose opinion really mattered told me, "You'll destroy your career staying over there, playing executive wife."

When I'm scared I drive, but I didn't drive in England. Stuart's company had given him a car and driver in London, but I couldn't call at midnight and say I wanted to tear off somewhere, up whatever road they had. When Stuart is scared, he builds up stores of chocolate bars and hides them. I didn't go looking for them, but there they were in the sock drawer. He knew I'd find them, and I did. It reminded me of my second husband half hiding his bottles, his way of saying 'I'm having a rough time and I'm not even going to try to talk about it.' Then I remembered what Trenton once told Stuart, so I did the opposite of what I felt like doing. I threw myself into bed. "I guess," I said, as I stroked his chin, "one of us has to walk naked through the snow."

The next day I thought of my parents and what they used to do when times were tense. Even during my father's busiest years, they'd take off for weekends alone out to Palm Springs or up to Santa Barbara. They'd put on their weekend personas and you'd sense their eagerness to split. My mother would sit in the car, straight and aloof, in one of her heavy silk sport shirts like Katharine Hepburn wore, with her gabardine slacks and little Tyrolean cardigans. My father, in his frontier outfit, would shut their suitcases in the trunk. They might not be talking when they left, but she'd be sitting snug, close to him when they came home.

We didn't talk on the drive up north. When we'd settled into our tower room, Stuart went out along the sea toward the castle. I started to write my kids, that turned into a chapter of something, the way letters do. Then I saw Stuart far out along the seaside path and I walked down the trail to meet him. I see us like a couple in a legend, coming toward each other down this long, jagged trail, each bearing a small packet of seeds we've searched for and finally found.

The first seed we carry is faith; the faith we each have, the ultimate essential during times when you're so scared you even hide from each other. Those times will come, so I try to remember when he's in serious pain he does have a force beyond chocolate. He knows I do, too.

The second seed is self-knowledge. You must know who you are. Maybe you can't help falling in love, but when you've worked hard, understanding yourself, you tend to fall for a copilot, not a passenger.

The third seed is grit. You must not have illusions about life's tough times. The best marriages combine strong individual characters who had been through enough, seen enough, to handle any compromise with patience and flair. When someone said, "For better or worse," they heard "worse," and knowing well what "worse" could mean, went right ahead.

Most people fight about sex and money, but those are really fear fights, too. Most people would put sex in the top three of their list of what matters in a marriage. Even if they both hate it, at least they've talked enough to agree about that. Sex is really all about 'I know you, you know me.' We know where we fit and how to realize each other's urgency with a passionate exchange.

Then money is a fear fight, too. Do I make enough money to make this work? Stuart and I haven't ever fought about it because we had a pretty fair idea of how we each really dealt with it when we met, and neither one of us had any illusions about our attitude toward it.

Then we have the seed of willingness, just in case grit gets confused with stubbornness. We know ourselves well enough to know how to turn around, to give and to change. Planted together, these seeds will grow. We will have sturdy roots in our world. We have a trust and commitment that branches out—a sheltering element for people we love.

I ran to him now and held him close. After time by the sea, I was ready to face London again, to be a steady partner—the writer and the writer, focusing on his work and my own.

I feel at home in the British Museum Reading Room, with comforting memories of undergraduate days and endless hours amid library stacks. The rustling of pages, the soft thud of falling books, coughs, blown noses, foot treads, whispers. I am lost in reveries, in another space and time, meeting Jill, falling in love, getting to know each other, marriage, and now this great adventure.

The pattern of our relationship is now so clear. We fell in love at first sight. Love happened to us: we didn't control it. But, then, we did try to control the hard part: the persistence in the commitment, the compromises, the walking the extra mile, and then another extra mile. Getting through the nitty-gritty while cherishing the kisses and the flowers. All so simple, and so demanding, and oh so rewarding.

I shake my head and look across the vast circular space of the Reading Room. In sharp focus, against a vague background of endless books, is a face. Jill, standing there, throwing me the penetrating look I saw that night we first met in the Connecticut diner. She comes slowly toward me until she is next to me at desk A9, underneath the Christian Biography sign.

"Would you like to come to my place for a cup of tea sometime?" she asks.

"Yes," I say, "right now would be good. Yes, oh yes."